BROADMAN COMMENTS

June 1999 - August 1999

BROADMAN COMMENTS

June 1999 - August 1999

13 User-Friendly Bible Study Lessons

ROBERT J. DEAN

WILLIAM E. ANDERSON

JAMES E. TAULMAN

BROADMAN
& HOLMAN
PUBLISHERS

Nashville, Tennessee

This material was published first in *Broadman Comments, 1998–1999*

© Copyright 1998 • Broadman and Holman Publishers
Nashville, Tennessee
All rights reserved

ISBN: 0–8054–1761–3

The Outlines of the International Sunday School Lessons, Uniform Series, are
copyrighted by the Committee on the Uniform Series and are used by permission.

Dewey Decimal Classification: 268.61
Subject Heading: SUNDAY SCHOOL LESSONS—COMMENTARIES

Broadman Comments *is published quarterly by Broadman & Holman Publishers,
127 Ninth Avenue, North, Nashville, Tennessee 37234*

*When ordered with other church literature, it sells for $5.99 per quarter.
Second class postage paid at Nashville, Tennessee*

ISSN: 0068–2721

POSTMASTER: Send address change to *Broadman Comments,*
Customer Service Center, 127 Ninth Avenue, North
Nashville, Tennessee 37234

Library of Congress Catalog Card Number: 45–437
Printed in the United States of America

WRITERS

STUDYING THE BIBLE

Robert J. Dean continues the theological traditions of *Broadman Comments* while adding his own fresh insights. Dean is retired from the Baptist Sunday School Board and is a Th.D. graduate of New Orleans Seminary.

APPLYING THE BIBLE

William E. Anderson has been pastor of Calvary Baptist Church, Clearwater, Florida, since 1975. Calvary's weekly services are telecast on various local stations and by satellite over Christian Network, Inc., on the Dish Network.

TEACHING THE BIBLE

James E. Taulman is a freelance writer in Nashville, Tennessee. Prior to that, Taulman was an editor of adult Sunday school materials for the Baptist Sunday School Board.

Scripture passages are from the authorized King James Version of the Bible.

Contents

Genesis: Beginnings

INTRODUCTION

The book of Genesis includes the first two periods of Old Testament history (beginnings and patriarchs). **Unit 1**, a four-lesson unit called "In the Beginning," deals with the period of beginnings. The first two lessons focus on God's good creation; the other two lessons describe sin, judgment, and grace as seen in Cain and Abel, and in Noah and the flood.

The other two units deal with the patriarchs. **Unit 2**, "The Beginnings of a People," is a four-lesson unit on Abraham's call, the birth of Isaac, the command to sacrifice Isaac, and the early life of Jacob.

Unit 3, "A People Tested," is a five-lesson unit on Jacob's encounter with God at Bethel, his later encounter at Peniel, the selling of Joseph by his brothers, his rise to power in Egypt, and his forgiveness and reconciliation with his brothers.

OUTLINE OF GENESIS

- I. **Period of Beginnings (1–11)**
  - A. **God's Good Creation (1–2)**
  - B. **Sin, Judgment, and Grace (3–11)**
    1. **Sin of Adam and Eve (3)**
    2. **Cain, Abel, and Seth (4–5)**
    3. **Noah, the Flood, and a New Beginning (6–10)**
    4. **The Tower of Babel and Its Consequences (11)**
- II. **Period of Patriarchs (12–50)**
  - A. **Abraham—Father of People of Faith (12–24)**
    1. **Journey to Canaan at God's Command (12)**
    2. **Problems Related to Lot (13–14)**
    3. **God's Promise and Abraham's Faith (15)**
    4. **God's Promise of a Son (16–17)**
    5. **Intercession for Sodom and Gomorrah (18–19)**
    6. **Birth of Isaac, Child of Promise (20–21)**
    7. **Ultimate Test of Abraham's Faith (22)**
    8. **Abraham Finds a Wife for Isaac (23–24)**
  - B. **Isaac—Man of Peace (25–27)**
    1. **Rivalry of Esau and Jacob (25)**
    2. **The Covenant Renewed with Isaac (26)**
    3. **The Blessing of Isaac Secured by Deception (27)**
  - C. **Jacob—from Supplanter to Saint (28–37)**
    1. **Encounter with God at Bethel (28)**
    2. **Haran: Work, Marriages, and Family (29–31)**
    3. **Encounter with God at Peniel (32)**
    4. **Reconciliation with Esau (33)**
    5. **Calling His Sinful Sons to Bethel (34–35)**
    6. **Loss of Rachel, Isaac, and Joseph (36–37)**
  - D. **Joseph—Faithful and Forgiving (38–50)**
    1. **Faithful to God in Potiphar's House (38)**
    2. **Faithful in Prison (39–40)**
    3. **Grain Administrator in Egypt (41)**
    4. **Reconciliation with His Brothers (42–45)**
    5. **Jacob and His Family in Egypt (46–49)**
    6. **Faith in Providence and Forgiveness for Others (50)**

Cycle of 1998–2004

1998–1999	1999–2000	2000–2001	2001–2002	2002–2003	2003–2004
Old Testament Survey	Exodus Leviticus Numbers Deuteronomy Joshua	Judges 1, 2 Samuel 1 Chronicles 1 Kings 1–11 2 Chronicles 1–9	Parables Miracles Sermon on the Mount	2 Kings 18–25 2 Chronicles 29–36 Jeremiah Lamentations Ezekiel Habakkuk Zephaniah	James 1, 2 Peter 1, 2, 3 John Jude
New Testament Survey	Matthew	Luke	Isaiah 9; 11; 40–66; Ruth Jonah Nahum	Personalities of the NT	Christmas Esther Job Ecclesiastes Song of Solomon
John	1, 2 Corinthians	Acts	Romans Galatians	Mark	The Cross 1, 2 Thessalonians Revelation
Genesis	Ephesians Philippians Colossians Philemon	1 Kings 12– 2 Kings 17 2 Chronicles 10–28 Isaiah 1–39 Amos Hosea Micah	Psalms Proverbs	Ezra Nehemiah Daniel Joel Obadiah Haggai Zechariah Malachi	Hebrews 1, 2 Timothy Titus

God's Good Creation

June

6

1999

Background Passage: Genesis 1:1–2:4a
Focal Passages: Genesis 1:1–2, 20–25, 29–31

Genesis means "beginning." The English title for the first book of the Bible comes from the Hebrew title, which uses the Hebrew word translated "in the beginning." It is indeed a book of beginnings. The foundations for the rest of the Bible are laid in Genesis, especially in the early chapters. The revelation of God as Creator of His good creation is a key foundation of faith. Taken as a whole, the book of Genesis describes the first two periods of Old Testament history: Beginnings and Patriarchs.

▶**Study Aim:** *To testify why they believe that God is Creator and that His creation is good.*

STUDYING THE BIBLE

OUTLINE AND SUMMARY
    I. **God the Creator (Gen. 1:1–2)**
        1. Eternal Creator of heaven and earth (1:1)
        2. Beginning of creation (1:2)
   II. **The Creation (Gen. 1:3–2:4a)**
        1. Orderly creation (1:3–19)
        2. All creatures small and great (1:20–28)
        3. The good God and His good creation (1:29–2:4a)

The eternal God is the Creator of the universe (1:1). The Spirit of God hovered over the face of the waters (1:2). God created light, heaven and earth, plants, sun and moon (1:3–19). God created living creatures: fish, birds, animals, and humans (1:20–28). The good God pronounced His creation very good (1:29–2:4a).

I. God the Creator (Gen. 1:1–2)
1. Eternal Creator of heaven and earth (1:1)
    1 In the beginning God created the heaven and the earth.

The Word of God does not seek to prove the existence of God. The biblical writers assumed the reality of God. As far as they were concerned, only a fool would say, "There is no God" (Ps. 14:1). The Bible begins by telling what God did. He revealed Himself by His actions.

He is revealed as eternal Creator of the universe. "Heaven and earth" refer to what we would call the universe—all things. The Hebrew word translated "created" in verse 1 always has God as its subject. It appears several times in Genesis 1:1–2:4a (1:1, 21, 27 [three times]; 2:3, 4).

The Hebrew word usually translated "God" is *elohim.* This is a plural word that sometimes means "gods" (Exod 12:12); however, when it refers to God, it usually appears with singular verbs. Some scholars believe that the use of this plural form shows that although God is one, He is not "one" in the sense that He can be confined to one way of revealing Himself. The Hebrew word for the God of Israel, *Yahweh,* does not appear until Genesis 2:4b. The more general word for God is appropriate for describing the creation, since all people have been created by God.

"In the beginning" does not mean God's beginning, but the beginning of the created universe. God Himself is "from everlasting to everlasting" (Ps. 90:2). The universe is not eternal, but it had a beginning. Having a beginning implies that it will have an ending. The rest of the Bible affirms that this is true. Many pagan people believed in a cyclical view of history and human existence. Humans are trapped within this recurring round-and-round of history and existence. However, God created the universe for a purpose; and He is moving it and humans toward His purpose.

2. Beginning of creation (1:2)

2 And the earth was without form, and void; and darkness was upon the face of the deep. And the Spirit of God moved upon the face of the waters.

The first part of verse 2 has perplexed Bible students. Does this refer to some preexisting material from which God formed the universe? Or does it refer to the first stage in the creation of the universe mentioned in verse 1? Most of us prefer the second view. Orthodox Christian doctrine is that only God is eternal; He created the universe out of nothing. He is Creator, not a manufacturer using existing raw materials.

"Darkness" is often a symbol of evil in the Bible (Isa. 5:20); however, this is not the case of the darkness that was part of God's good creation. "I form the light, and create darkness" (Isa. 45:7). God is not the author of evil, but of good (Jas. 1:13–17). It is true that when God made humans with free choice, evil became a possibility; and when they sinned, evil became a reality. However, God does not create evil.

The word translated "spirit" can also mean "wind" or "breath." In a sense, the Spirit of God is the breath or wind of God. "Moved upon" is the same word used in Deuteronomy 32:11 to describe how an eagle hovers over its young.

II. The Creation (Gen. 1:3–2:4a)

1. Orderly creation (1:3–19)

The biblical account next summarizes the orderliness of creation. First, God created light (1:3–5). Second, He created what we would call heaven and earth; He also created seeds and plants (1:6–13). Third, God created the sun and moon (1:14–19). These events took place during what the Bible calls the first three days of creation. In those days God created a habitable earth. Then in the next three days God created living things to dwell on that earth.

2. All creatures small and great (1:20–28)

20 And God said, Let the waters bring forth abundantly the moving creature that hath life, and fowl that may fly above the earth in the open firmament of heaven.

21 And God created great whales, and every living creature that moveth, which the waters brought forth abundantly,

after their kind, and every winged fowl after his kind: and God saw that it was good.

22 And God blessed them, saying, Be fruitful, and multiply, and fill the waters in the seas, and let fowl multiply in the earth.

23 And the evening and the morning were the fifth day.

24 And God said, Let the earth bring forth the living creature after his kind, cattle, and creeping thing, and beast of the earth after his kind: and it was so.

25 And God made the beast of the earth after his kind, and cattle after their kind, and every thing that creepeth upon the earth after his kind: and God saw that it was good.

After having created a habitable earth, God created "every living creature." He created fish and birds (1:20–23). Then He made land animals (1:24–25). Then God created humans in His own image. God had told the animals to be fruitful and multiply; He gave the same commission to humans. However, God also made humans stewards over the rest of creation (1:26–28; since we will look at "God's Purpose for People" on June 13, we will save further comments until then.)

Three things stand out in Genesis 1:3–31, which are illustrated in verses 20–28. (1) First of all, the method of divine creation is seen in the repeated theme, "And God said." This crucial statement is found 10 times (1:3, 6, 9, 11, 14, 20, 24, 26, 28, 29). This is the Bible's way of describing the *how* of divine creation. He created by the power of His word. In ancient times, words meant more than they do today. Words were extensions of a person's personality. This is especially true of the word of the eternal God. He simply spoke the word, and various parts of the creation came into being.

(2) Closely related to "and God said" is the clause "and it was so" (1:7, 9, 11, 15, 24, 30). This is another way of making the same point as the words, "Let there be light: and there was light" (1:3). When God spoke a creative word, it happened as He said.

(3) Another theme is the goodness of God's creation. Notice how often you read the words, "And God saw that it was good" (1:10, 12, 18, 21, 25). This leads up to God's final appraisal of His completed work, "And God saw . . . it was very good" (1:31). We will say more about this when we get to verse 31. The word *blessed* in verses 22 and 28 is another indication of God's goodness.

From the perspective of the Hebrews, some of the living creatures were frightening. Hebrews were not usually a seafaring people. Therefore, whales seemed "great" indeed to them. However, the passage shows that these are only "great" from a human perspective. They are creatures of the sovereign God, who made them all good.

People who live close to the land have a feel for the interrelation of living things and even nature itself that other humans seem to lack. Some people have misinterpreted the divine command to have dominion that God gave to humans (1:28) as justification for exploiting God's good creation for their own purposes. Actually, God was calling humans to exercise faithful stewardship over the rest of creation in the name of the Creator.

3. The good God and His good creation (1:29–2:4a)

29 And God said, Behold, I have given you every herb bearing seed, which is upon the face of all the earth, and every tree in the which is the fruit of a tree yielding seed; to you it shall be for meat.

30 And to every beast of the earth, and to every fowl of the air, and to every thing that creepeth upon the earth, wherein there is life, I have given every green herb for meat: and it was so.

31 And God saw every thing that he had made, and, behold, it was very good. And the evening and the morning were the sixth day.

God not only created living things, but He also made provision for their food. The word translated "meat" is a more general word for food. In God's original good creation, humans and other living things were to eat only plants. Thus the picture in Genesis 2:19 of Adam naming the animals depicts a paradise in which all living creatures lived in harmony and peace.

God looked at His finished work of creation and pronounced it "very good." The creation reveals God's power and wisdom. The fact that He created, blessed, and sustained His good creation also testifies to the goodness of God Himself.

One of the most controversial parts of Genesis 1 has been the meaning of the word *day* as used for the six days of creation. Some Bible-believing Christians understand these to have been twenty-four-hour days. Other Bible-believing Christians think these "days" may represent longer periods of time. The latter group points out that the sun and moon were not created until the fourth "day" (1:14). Also the whole period of creation is called a "day" in Genesis 2:4b. Humans are time-bound creatures, but the eternal God has no such restrictions on Him. "One day is with the LORD as a thousand years, and a thousand years as one day" (2 Pet. 3:8).

We live in a world in which many people seek to explain the universe only as a physical phenomenon, with no divine Creator having anything to do with it. Hebrews 11:3 states a basic tenet of biblical faith, "Through faith we understand that the worlds were framed by the word of God." This is the real battle line that separates those who believe in divine creation from those who believe in a purely naturalistic origin of the universe. As far as people of faith in God are concerned, it would take more blind gullibility to believe that the universe just happened than to believe that a wise, powerful Creator called it into being in ways beyond human understanding.

This is certainly a more satisfying kind of faith than the faith in naturalistic processes unguided by any overseeing God. In a candid moment, one of the advocates of naturalism admitted that human beings are alone in the midst of a vast, uncaring universe. Personally, I had rather live with the trust that our lives and universe are in the hands of the good God, who called the good creation into being. His purpose for us and our universe is good. We can entrust ourselves to Him, even though we cannot explain Him and His ways (Isa. 55:8–9).

Genesis 2:1–4a pictures God resting from His creative work. This is the kind of rest that comes with the completion of a satisfying task. It does not indicate that God became inactive and left His creations to fend for themselves. The rest of the Bible shows His continuing involvement with His creation. After sin came, He continued to work for good by offering a way of salvation. And the final chapters of Revelation picture a restoration of the original purpose of God's good creation.

SUMMARY OF BIBLE TRUTHS

1. The Bible doesn't seek to prove the existence of God; it affirms what He did as Creator.
2. God's creative word called all things into being.
3. God's creation is good.
4. God not only created the universe, but He continued to sustain living things.
5. Although we cannot understand God and His ways, we can trust Him as wise, powerful, and good.
6. Faith in God as Creator is more believable and more satisfying than believing purely naturalistic explanations of the universe.

APPLYING THE BIBLE

1. Right from the top down. I grew up in a family of eight children and my brother-in-law and sister, my surrogate parents, rarely quarrelled. I have thought, since becoming a parent of four, that they didn't quarrel, more than likely, simply because of a lack of energy. In any case, I distinctly remember "The Quarrel." My brother-in-law believed he could do anything anybody else could do, including those things he had no experience whatever in doing, such as paperhanging. After he and my sister had made a fiasco of the attempt to re-paper our living room, and had argued heatedly several times in the process, he relented, swallowed his pride (a Herculean task!), and hired a man who, by himself, and with a pegleg, did a beautiful job of papering our living room—for a pittance. When he was through, my brother-in-law asked him where he had gone wrong and the man gave away a trade secret: one must begin the "hang" at the top of the wall, at the ceiling, and let the pre-cut piece of paper fall slowly into its place along the wall. The key, he said, was to get it started right at the top. If that went wrong, I remember him saying, nothing else could go right. And such a mistake, he said, could only be corrected by taking the paper down and starting again.

If we get the matter of God creating the universe wrong, nothing else can ever go right. It's where everything begins, and it is critical that we get beginnings right. In fact, many argue that the matter of God's special creation—both of the universe and man—is the most important doctrine in the entire Bible.

2. Highly unlikely. In his book *Energy Flow in Biology,* Harold Morowitz estimates the probability for the chance formation of the smallest and simplest form of living organism we know. It would occur one in 10 raised to the 340,000,000th power, or, to say it another way, there would be one chance in the number one followed by 340 million zeros. Vastly more faith is required to believe what naturalistic science proposes about the origin of the universe than what God says about it.

3. A miracle by another name. "Fred Hoyle has become famous because (a metaphor he used) vividly conveys the magnitude of the problem (of creation by chance): that a living organism emerged by chance from a pre-biotic soup is about as likely as that 'a tornado sweeping through a junkyard might assemble a Boeing 747 from the materials therein.' Chance assembly is just a naturalistic way of saying 'miracle.' Hoyle has long been recognized as one of the world's top mathematical astrophysicists, and he has authored many books on the origin of the universe.)

4. God's orderly universe. A children's book appeared some time ago in which an imaginary planet is described where everything happens unpredictably. The sun rises one day, but doesn't the next. And if it does, it might appear at any hour of the "day." On some days the moon might come up instead of the sun, and vice versa. One day water would boil at one temperature and on another day, at another temperature. One day you might be able to jump up and down on the surface of the earth, and on another, gravity might be so strong that you couldn't jump at all. And so on. The point is this: God created an orderly universe, with very predictable laws. Does that matter? One result is that science, which is so often seen as an enemy of the Christian faith, can occur, and can only occur, in the universe Genesis describes. To put it another way: Leading scientists admit that only in a Judeo-Christian context could modern science arise. Or to quote Einstein: "God did not play dice with the universe."

5. Truth that passes understanding. A man often said he couldn't believe the Bible because he did not understand how all that is written in it could be true. It was, he said, simply beyond his capability to understand. Some time later he was walking on the beach. He saw a little boy dig a hole in the sand and then begin to pour sea water into the hole. The man watched him for a while and then asked him what he was doing. "I am going to pour the ocean into this hole," the lad replied. The man laughed at the boy's impossible task, only to see the boy turn into an angel who asked the man: "Do you think God can put all He knows into your finite mind?"

6. For discussion:

▶ Does it really matter that we accept the fact of God's special creation of the universe? What effect does the issue have on morals and ethics?

▶ If we are but highly advanced apes, how can we be held responsible for ape-like behavior?

▶ If death is simply a natural phenomenon with no moral overtones at all, what do we do with the doctrine of death as sin's punishment, which the Bible everywhere states?

‣ If the evolutionists are right that the highest law is "the survival of the fittest," what about helping the poor and the sick and the crippled and the weak? Isn't that a violation of the order of nature?
‣ How could we ever say that Jesus is divine since He, too, according to the evolutionist, is fully man and therefore but a highly- dvanced ape?
‣ How can there be such a thing as an eternal judgment if, again, there can be no basis for moral discussion since we are but animals?
‣ Could it be that the unprecedented violence and anger and hardness which is manifest in the world today has some connection with the last couple of generations of children being taught the doctrine of evolution and not of special divine creation?

TEACHING THE BIBLE

‣ *Main Idea:* God's creation is good.
‣ *Suggested Teaching Aim:* To lead adults to testify why they believe that God is Creator and that His creation is good.

A TEACHING OUTLINE

God's Good Creation

1. *God the Creator (Gen. 1:1–2)*
2. *The Creation (Gen. 1:3–2:4a)*

Introduce the Bible Study

Use introduction #1, "Right from the top down," from "Applying the Bible" to introduce the lesson. Say, Today's lesson will help us get the matter straight from the top.

Search for Biblical Truth

IN ADVANCE, copy the thirteen lesson titles and dates on a large sheet of paper. Mount this on a wall where you can leave it all quarter. Make a large arrow out of colored paper and move it each week to highlight the lesson being studied.

Ask, According to Genesis 1:1, how does the Bible seek to prove the existence of God? (It doesn't; God's existence is a given.) Why do you think the biblical writers did not seek to prove God's existence?

Ask members to look at Genesis 1:1–2:4a and count the number of times "created" is used in these verses. (Seven times in KJV: 1:1, 21, 27 [3 times]; 2:3, 4.)

Ask members to look at 1:1–2:4a and find what name is used to describe God. (God=Elohim.) Now ask them to look at 2:4b-25 and find what name is used in that section. (Lord God=Yahweh.) Say, The more general word for God (Elohim) is appropriate for describing the creation since all people have been created by God; the word translated "Lord God" is the covenant name for God, which God revealed to the Hebrews.

Read this statement and ask members why they agree or disagree with it: "God is Creator, not a manufacturer using existing raw materials." Ask, If God created all things, did He also create evil? Why? (See "Studying the Bible.")

Ask, How did God create? (By His word.) Ask members to search 1:1–31 to find how many times the phrase "And God said" appears. (Ten times in KJV: 1:3, 6, 9, 11, 14, 20, 24, 26, 28, 29.) Ask members to search 1:1–31 and count the number of times the phrase "And God saw that it was good" appears (five times in KJV: 1:10, 12, 18, 21, 25.) Ask, How does 1:31 differ? (*Very* good.)

Prepare a brief lecture in which you state the following three ways Christians think the word *day* is used in 1:1–2:4: (1) Twenty-four-hour day; (2) represents a period of time; (3) Used in 2:4b to refer to the whole period of creation. Quote: "Humans are time-bound creatures, but the eternal God has no such restrictions on Him."

Ask, How can we know that God created the universe? Ask a volunteer to read Hebrews 11:3. Share the information in illustrations #2 and #3 from "Applying the Bible."

Read aloud the six summary statements in "Summary of Bible Truths." Ask members to listen for one statement that particularly helps them explain why they believe God is the Creator and that His creation is good.

Give the Truth a Personal Focus

Say, We may not understand everything about creation, but we do not need to. Share the story in #5 from "Applying the Bible." Point out that God really is not through with creation because He continues to create new life in us. Close in prayer that all members will experience God's creative power in their lives.

---

1. H. J. Morowitz, *Energy Flow in Biology* (New York: Academic Press, 1968), 99.
2. Phillip Johnson, *Darwin on Trial* (Washington, D.C.: Regnery Gateway, 1991), 104.

God's Purpose for People

Background Passage: Genesis 2:4–25
Focal Passages: Genesis 2:7–9,15–25

Genesis 2:4–25 supplements the account of creation in Genesis 1:1–2:3. Genesis 1:26–28 summarized the creation of humans in God's image, entrusting them with stewardship over the rest of creation and making them co-creators with God of new human life. Genesis 2:4–25 provides additional insight into God's purpose in creating man and woman.

▶**Study Aim:** *To identify aspects of God's purpose for human relationships, work, and marriage.*

STUDYING THE BIBLE

OUTLINE AND SUMMARY

  I. **Man and the Garden (Gen. 2:4–17)**
  1. **Creation of man (2:4–7)**
  2. **Garden of Eden (2:8–14)**
  3. **Man's work and freedom of choice (2:15–17)**
 II. **Man, Woman, and Marriage (Gen. 2:18–25)**
  1. **Man's need for companionship (2:18–20)**
  2. **Creation of woman (2:21–23)**
  3. **God's purpose for marriage (2:24–25)**

God gave man the gift of life (2:4–7). The Lord put the man in the beautiful garden of Eden (2:8–14). Man was to take care of the garden and enjoy all its fruits, but he was forbidden to eat of the tree of the knowledge of good and evil (2:15–17). Since it was not good for the man to be alone, God planned to provide a helper suitable for him (2:18–20). God created woman and brought her to Adam (2:21–23). Marriage is to be a one-flesh union of husband and wife that supersedes all other human relationships (2:24–25).

I. Man and the Garden (Gen. 2:4–17)

1. Creation of man (2:4–7)

> **7 And the LORD God formed man of the dust of the ground, and breathed into his nostrils the breath of life; and man became a living soul.**

Genesis 2:4 is the first appearance of a formula using the words "these are the generations of" that divides the book into sections (5:1; 6:9; 10:1; 11:10, 27; 25:12; 25:19; 36:9; 37:2). Rain had not fallen, but a mist rose up to water the plants (2:5–6).

God created man from the dust of the ground and breathed into him the breath of life. Although we sometimes forget it, life is purely the gift of God. This was true of the first human, and it is true of all who are born of human parents as co-creators of life with God. The words translated "living soul" in verse 7 are the same words translated "living creature" in Genesis 1:21, 24; 9:10. The Hebrew words mean "living being." Although these same words are used of all to whom God gave the gift of life, the uniqueness of the man was in his being created in God's image—with a capacity for fellowship with God.

2. Garden of Eden (2:8–14)

8 And the LORD God planted a garden eastward in Eden; and there he put the man whom he had formed.

9 And out of the ground made the LORD God to grow every tree that is pleasant to the sight, and good for food; the tree of life also in the midst of the garden, and the tree of knowledge of good and evil.

God had already created plant life, but He caused a number of kinds of trees to grow in the garden. The description of all of them as pleasing to look at and good to eat is repeated in Genesis 3:6, as Eve was being tempted. The tempter suggested to Eve that God was being stingy with her and Adam; however, Genesis 2:9 clearly shows how false was that charge.

Two special trees are mentioned for the first time in verse 9. Both play crucial parts in events that follow. One was the tree of life. The other tree was the tree of knowledge of good and evil. Four rivers watered the garden, including two we recognize: the Tigris and the Euphrates (2:10–14). Gold and other precious stones are mentioned in verses 11–12, further evidence of God's goodness and bounty offered to humankind.

3. Man's work and freedom of choice (2:15–17)

15 And the LORD God took the man, and put him into the garden of Eden to dress it and to keep it.

The word translated "dress" is the usual word for "work," although at times the work has the connotation of service. The word translated "keep" means "take care of." These are key words that undergird two key biblical doctrines: work and stewardship. God created useful and satisfying work as part of His good creation. God is a worker, and He made man to work. After sin came, fulfilling work became grinding toil (Gen. 3:17–19).

Stewardship of man over the rest of creation was mentioned first in 1:26, 28. Here it is reinforced by God giving man the oversight of the garden. He was to be God's trustee to work and care for the garden. Thus, the garden was not only a blessing but also a trust from God.

16 And the LORD God commanded the man, saying, Of every tree of the garden thou mayest freely eat:

17 But of the tree of the knowledge of good and evil, thou shalt not eat of it: for in the day that thou eatest thereof thou shalt surely die.

These verses reveal two other crucial facts about human beings. One is that God made humans as persons capable of fellowship with God. Notice that God addresses the man as "thou." This shows that man was a person, not an animal. And it shows that he was a person with whom God spoke. This is a big part of what was meant in Genesis 1:26–27 about being created in God's image. God is a person; so was the man He created.

Of huge importance is the fact that God gave the man the freedom to choose to obey God or to disobey Him. The tree of the knowledge of good and evil signified this important fact. Here is another significant difference between man and the animals. They are creatures whose actions are governed by instinct. Man, however, is capable of making moral choices.

Some people make light of the sin of eating the forbidden fruit in Genesis 3. They ask, "What's so bad about eating some forbidden fruit?" What was so bad was that this was a test of whether man would love, trust, and obey God.

The Bible never clearly explains why God gave man that terrible freedom. As God, He didn't have to make humans with freedom of choice. He could have made creatures that were designed or programmed always to do what He said. The most likely answer is that God made us free because love is possible only in an atmosphere of freedom. Robots cannot be programmed to love. Only free creatures can choose to love. In order to be free to love God, people must be free to reject His love.

II. Man, Woman, and Marriage (Gen. 2:18–25)
1. Man's need for companionship (2:18–20)

18 And the LORD God said, It is not good that the man should be alone; I will make him an help meet for him.

19 And out of the ground the LORD God formed every beast of the field, and every fowl of the air; and brought them unto Adam to see what he would call them: and whatsoever Adam called every living creature, that was the name thereof.

20 And Adam gave names to all cattle, and to the fowl of the air, and to every beast of the field; but for Adam there was not found an help meet for him.

Chapter 1 repeatedly used the word *good* to describe various parts of God's creation; however, Genesis 2:18 describes something that was "not good." It was "not good for man to be alone." Man was made for companionship. This is a negative way of saying that humans are social beings. People need God, but they also need people. To put it another way, community was part of God's original plan for humans. Marriage became the foundation for the family, which is the primary building block of community.

Specifically, the man needed a "help meet." These words in Hebrew mean "a helper suitable for him." "Suitable" means literally "like what is in front of him." "Helper" is one who aids and supports. All the animals were paraded past the man. As they passed by, he named them. This was a sign of his stewardship over them. He had the authority to name them. However, none of the three categories of animals—domestic, birds, and wild animals—provided a suitable helper for Adam.

Notice that the name *Adam* appears in the King James Version first in verse 19. The Hebrew word for man used up to this point is *adam*. At times, *adam* has a definite article "the man"; at other times, it is simply "man." We know from Genesis 5:1–3 that the man was an individual eventually called Adam. Translators differ about the point at which *adam* should be translated as a proper name. Adam was an individual; yet in a sense Adam stood for everyman.

2. Creation of woman (2:21–23)

21 And the LORD God caused a deep sleep to fall upon Adam, and he slept; and he took one of his ribs, and closed up the flesh instead thereof.

22 And the rib, which the LORD God had taken from man, made he a woman, and brought her unto the man.

23 And Adam said, This is now bone of my bones, and flesh of my flesh; she shall be called Woman, because she was taken out of Man.

God created a helper suitable for the man by creating a woman. God Himself performed surgery on Adam and created woman from one of Adam's ribs. After God had done this, He "brought her unto the man." The latter clause pictures God bringing them together to fulfill man's need for a companion.

Verse 23 contains the first words of Adam that the Bible records. Significantly, his words were words of wonder and gratitude for the woman God had brought to him. What he had not found among any of the animals, Adam recognized in the woman. She was like him, but she was in some ways different from him. Together they found fulfillment in each other. If we were paraphrasing the emotional response of Adam when he first saw the woman, we might say, "Wonderful, she's just what I've been looking for!"

3. God's purpose for marriage (2:24–25)

24 Therefore shall a man leave his father and his mother, and shall cleave unto his wife: and they shall be one flesh.

25 And they were both naked, the man and his wife, and were not ashamed.

Verse 24 states the biblical foundation for marriage and sex. Both were part of God's original good creation. Jesus quoted Genesis 2:24 as God's original intention for marriage (Matt. 19:3–9; Mark 10:2–12). Jesus interpreted marriage to be the lifetime union of one man and one woman joined in one-flesh union. Paul also quoted the verse as a sign of the spiritual union between Christ and the church (Eph. 5:31). And he cited it to show that sexual immorality is wrong because it is a perversion of God's intention for sex (1 Cor. 6:16).

"One flesh" refers to more than sex. It includes the oneness of companionship and endeavors that a couple shares. Neither loses individuality, but they find a wholeness in each other. Although "one flesh" includes more than sex, it surely includes sexual relations. Nothing is said in Genesis 2:24 about procreation. We know from Genesis 1:26 that becoming parents is one purpose of sex in marriage; yet it is not the only purpose (see Prov. 5:15–19; 1 Cor. 7:2–5).

This explains why sexual relations outside of marriage are sinful. Sex was a gift of God so that a man and a woman could express total commitment to each other in a responsible and lasting relationship. People who have sex outside of marriage are playing with fire. They are misusing the ultimate means of human bonding. Sex is designed to be enjoyed in an atmosphere of total commitment and unquestioning trust. This is one reason why the man and his wife were not ashamed to be naked. They were making themselves completely vulnerable to each other.

Marriage creates a new relationship that takes precedence over all other relationships. The Hebrews placed special importance on honoring parents; yet when a couple married, their first loyalty was to each other. This is the significance of the word *leave* in verse 24. Of course, this verse was looking to the future of humanity. Adam had no father and mother to leave, but his descendants would have human parents.

SUMMARY OF BIBLE TRUTHS

1. Man was offered bountiful blessings by God.
2. Man was created a person capable of fellowship with God.
3. Man was given a choice to obey or disobey God.
4. Work, community, marriage, and sex were part of God's good creation.
5. People need the companionship of other people.
6. God intends marriage to be a lifetime union of one man and one woman.

APPLYING THE BIBLE

1. One too many! "There are many examples of psychopaths who do not kill, but do spread hurt around. One such man is Giovanni Vigliotto. Henderson writes that Vigliotto was sent to prison for marrying 105 wives, without divorcing the others. (That is bigamy taken to cosmic proportions!) His mistake was with wife number 104. Sharon Clark may have been foolish enough to fall for him, but she wasn't about to let it drop when he ran off with all her money and possessions. Unlike the other 103 before her, she tracked him down. Five states and another wife later, she caught up with him."[1] Solomon had a thousand wives and concubines, but he was not an imposter like Mr. Vigliotto. They both had more wives than God envisioned when he made a marriage of one man and one woman for the one man . . . forever!

2. How important is the home? "The family is an embryonic school, a more important educational institution than the school. It is an embryonic state, a more important institution for law and order than the state. It is also an embryonic church, a more basically determinative religious institution than the church."[2]

3. Others suffer because of our sins. Shakespeare puts this prayer into the mouth of the Duke of Clarence:

> "O God! If my deep prayers cannot appease;
> But thou wilt be aveng'd on my misdeeds,
> Yet execute thy wrath in me alone,

O, spare my guiltless wife and my poor children."
(*Richard III,* Act 2, Scene iv)

Most of us have prayed a prayer like that at one time or another. But, of course, God never answered that prayer for the Duke of Clarence, for Adam, or for anybody else! Those around us must suffer because of our sins.

4. Quick Quotes.

▶ "Just looking for loopholes!" (W. C. Fields during his last illness, to a shocked visitor who found him reading his Bible).[3]

▶ "Everybody soon or late sits down to a banquet of consequences" (Robert Louis Stevenson).

5. The decline of the family. Columnist Charles Krauthammer said, "The entire political spectrum agrees that the (American) family disintegration is at the heart of all our societal ills, but there doesn't seem to be much the federal government can do about it."[4] Discuss these questions: In your view, is the American family disintegrating? If so, why does that fact have a negative effect on the culture? Does the family unit really matter that much? Would living by the principles God established for the original family help the situation? Could it be successfully argued that our cultural setting is so different that biblical principles, established thousands of years ago, are simply not-applicable today? Is it the federal government's place to "do something about it?" What, specifically, can the church do to help strengthen modern families? What is the biblical perspective on today's "alternative life-tyles" in marriage?

TEACHING THE BIBLE

▶ *Main Idea:* God's purpose for the people He created included human relationships, work, and marriage.

▶ *Suggested Teaching Aim:* To lead adults to identify God's plan for human relationships, work, and marriage.

A TEACHING OUTLINE

God's Chosen People

1. *Man and the Garden (Gen. 2:4–17)*
2. *Man, Woman, and Marriage (Gen. 2:18–25)*

Introduce the Bible Study

Use number #1 from "Applying the Bible" to introduce the Bible study.

Search for Biblical Truth

Move the pointer on the quarter poster to highlight today's lesson. **IN ADVANCE,** organize members in three groups and assign one of these topics to each group: human relationships, work, or marriage. Give all members a sheet of paper and a pencil for them to make notes. Ask groups (1) to listen during the lesson for information and ideas about their subject and (2) to be prepared to share that information with the rest of the class at the end of the lesson.

IN ADVANCE, copy the six statements in "Summary of Bible Truths" on six large poster strips and place these around the room. Assign each person in the class one of the strips. (If you have more than six persons, you can assign more than one person to a statement; if you have fewer than six persons, you can assign some persons more than one strip.) Ask members to listen throughout the lesson to find a Scripture verse(s) that will support their statement.

IN ADVANCE, write "Life is purely the gift of God" on a sheet of paper and place it on the wall. Ask a volunteer to read 2:7. Ask, What made the man unique of all God's creatures? (Capacity for fellowship with God.)

Ask members to scan 2:8–9 and identify four characteristics of the trees God planted in the garden. (Pleasant to sight, good for food, tree of life, tree of good and evil.)

Ask members to scan 2:15–17 and answer: What tasks did God assigned to the man? (Dress and keep the garden.) What differences do these verses point out between man and the rest of God's creation? (God communicates with man.) Why did God give the man freedom to choose? Why was eating the forbidden fruit wrong?

DISCUSS: Is it possible for love to exist outside an atmosphere of freedom?

Ask members to scan 2:18–20 and identify something that was not good. (Not good for man to be alone.) What implications does this have for our lives? (Community was part of God's original plan.) What was the significance of Adam's naming the animals? (Stewardship of them.)

Ask members to scan 2:21–23 and find the first words Adam spoke. Distribute paper and pencils and ask members to put in their words what Adam said when he saw Eve.

Ask members to look at 2:24–25 and identify the verbs or action words in these two verses. (Leave, cleave, be, were) Ask, Based on these verses, what are God's requirements for marriage? (Leave, cleave, and be one flesh.) What is God's intention for husbands and wives relating to each other as sexual beings? (Naked but not ashamed.) What does "one flesh" mean? What does it say about individuality? Why were the man and woman not ashamed?

Read the six summary statements you have taped to the wall and ask members to suggest appropriate Scriptures. (Members may suggest other Scriptures, but consider these: **1**=2:16; **2**=2:17; **3**=2:17; **4**=2:15, 18, 24–25; **5**=2:18; **6**=2:24.)

Give the Truth a Personal Focus

Ask assigned groups to share information and ideas about their subject. Ask: What are some principles for human relationships? work? marriage? How can you apply these to your lives tomorrow?

1. Magid and McKelvey, *High Risk* (New York: Bantam Books, New York, 1987), 44.
2. T. B. Maston, *Christianity and World Issues* (New York: Macmillan, 1964), 63–64.
3. Quoted in *Forbes,* 16 April 1990, p. 24.
4. From an interview with Larry King, on *Larry King Live,* 3 May 1995.

Consequences of Sin

Background Passage: Genesis 4:1–26
Focal Passage: Genesis 4:1–16

During the survey of the Old Testament, we studied Genesis 3 (Sept. 6, 1998). That key chapter showed how sin separated us from God and from others. The story of Cain and Abel shows how these consequences were experienced in the first home.

▶**Study Aim:** *To describe Cain's sins and their consequences.*

STUDYING THE BIBLE

OUTLINE AND SUMMARY
    I. **Cain and Abel (Gen. 4:1–16)**
        1. **The gift of life (4:1–2)**
        2. **Acceptable and unacceptable worship (4:3–5)**
        3. **Anger and murder (4:6–8)**
        4. **Condemnation (4:9–12)**
        5. **Punishment (4:13–16)**
   II. **Cain's Descendants (Gen. 4:17–24)**
  III. **Birth of Seth (Gen. 4:25–26)**

God gave Adam and Eve two sons, Cain and Abel (4:1–2). Both brought offerings to God, but Abel was accepted and Cain was not (4:3–5). Cain failed to heed God's warning about his anger, and he murdered his brother (4:6–8). When Cain denied his guilt, God pronounced his condemnation (4:9–12). When Cain complained that someone might kill him, God placed Cain's life under divine protection (4:13–16). Cain's descendants showed some progress in material things, but sin became worse (4:17–24). The line of faith, begun in Abel, was continued through Seth and Enos (4:25–26).

I. Cain and Abel (Gen. 4:1–16)

1. The gift of life (4:1–2)

> **1 And Adam knew Eve his wife; and she conceived, and bare Cain, and said, I have gotten a man from the LORD.**
>
> **2 And she again bare his brother Abel. And Abel was a keeper of sheep, but Cain was a tiller of the ground.**

"Knew" is used in a variety of ways. It meant "to know intellectually," "to be acquainted," and "to experience." The word is also used in the Old Testament to describe the most intimate kind of knowledge—human sexual intercourse. It is never used to describe the same thing in animals. Adam and Eve obeyed the command to be fruitful and multiply (1:28). Eve conceived and bore a son.

When Cain was born, Eve exclaimed, "I have gotten a man from the LORD." She recognized that she was a co-creator of life with the Creator. Some Bible students think that her words also reflect her hope that her son was the seed of the woman promised in Genesis 3:15. Events proved him to be a very different kind of person.

When their second son was born, Eve named him Abel. The name has some kinship with the Hebrew word for "breath." Thus, it may signify life as a gift from God. And it may also signify the uncertainty of human life. Cain became a farmer, and Abel became a shepherd.

2. Acceptable and unacceptable worship (4:3–5)

3 And in process of time it came to pass, that Cain brought of the fruit of the ground an offering unto the LORD.

4 And Abel, he also brought of the firstlings of his flock and of the fat thereof. And the LORD had respect unto Abel and to his offering:

5 But unto Cain and to his offering he had not respect. And Cain was very wroth, and his countenance fell.

Here is evidence of the uniqueness of humans made in God's image. Humans have a capacity and a hunger for God. Thus Cain and Abel not only worked but also worshiped. Genesis 4 does not clearly explain why God was pleased with Abel and his offering but displeased with Cain and his offering.

Three explanations have been made: (1) Abel offered the best of his flocks. The word "firstlings" makes this clear. No such word is used of Cain's offerings. (2) Abel offered blood sacrifices, which were more acceptable to God. (3) The first two explanations focus on the offerings. The third focuses on the worshipers. Abel was a man of faith, whose worship was an expression of his faith (Heb. 11:4; see also 1 John 3:12). Cain's anger was probably directed both at God and at Abel. Perhaps God was dissatisfied with both the offering of Cain and Cain himself. Verse 5 mentions both.

The word translated "wroth" means literally "it became hot to him." He was angry, and his anger showed when his face fell.

3. Anger and murder (4:6–8)

6 And the LORD said unto Cain, Why art thou wroth? and why is thy countenance fallen?

7 If thou doest well, shalt thou not be accepted? and if thou doest not well, sin lieth at the door. And unto thee shall be his desire, and thou shalt rule over him.

8 And Cain talked with Abel his brother: and it came to pass, when they were in the field, that Cain rose up against Abel his brother, and slew him.

Verse 6 records the first of several questions that God asked Cain. God asked Cain why he was angry. His anger was wrong and dangerous, but it was not too late for Cain to change his attitude. God promised that Cain, too, would be accepted if he did. This implies that the reason for his being rejected was his sinful attitude toward God and Abel.

God, however, issued a solemn warning to Cain. If he did not get control of his anger, it would take control of him. The word *lieth* can be translated "crouches." The picture is of anger crouching like a wild animal at the door of Cain's heart. If Cain continued to pamper and feed his anger, the wild animal would be unleashed to do its worst. That seems to be the meaning of the last part of verse 7. "Its desire is for you, but you must master it" (NASB). Jesus said that anger in one's heart is comparable to murder (Matt. 5:21–22). Jesus did not mean that anger is as bad as actually murdering someone. However, He did mean that anger is sinful and that it can lead to murder.

Some old translations of verse 8 add these words to explain what Cain said to Abel, "Let us go into the field." The Hebrew text, however, doesn't tell us what Cain said to Abel. It does tell us what Cain did when the two were in the field. Cain murdered Abel his brother. The words "his brother" add to the horror.

4. Condemnation (4:9–12)

9 And the LORD said unto Cain, Where is Abel thy brother? And he said, I know not: Am I my brother's keeper?

Compare God's question to Cain in verse 9 with His question to Adam and Eve in Genesis 3:9. In neither case was God asking in order to get information He did not have. He knew where Adam and Eve were, and He knew what Cain had done. The purpose of the questions was to give them an opportunity to confess and to turn to Him. Adam's initial answer to God was an unsuccessful attempt at evasion (Gen. 3:10). Cain's answer was an outright lie.

Cain answered God's question with a denial and a question. He denied knowing where Abel was. Then he asked defiantly, "Am I my brother's keeper?" Cain obviously was not Abel's keeper in the sense of knowing where he was and what he was doing at all times. However, he was his keeper in the sense of being responsible for treating Abel as a brother.

10 And he said, What hast thou done? the voice of thy brother's blood crieth unto me from the ground.

11 And now art thou cursed from the earth, which hath opened her mouth to receive thy brother's blood from thy hand.

12 When thou tillest the ground, it shall not henceforth yield unto thee her strength; a fugitive and a vagabond shalt thou be in the earth.

God asked Cain the same question he had asked Eve in Genesis 3:13. "What have you done?" expressed God's horror at what Cain had done, his attempt at deception, and his unconcern for his brother's life. Cain may have thought that his sin was done in the field with no one watching, but God told him that his brother's blood was crying out from the ground to God. Sin is not something that we can hide. This is not only because God sees all that we do but also because sin itself carries the seeds of the condemnation of the sinner. "Be sure your sin will find you out" (Num. 32:23; see also Gal. 6:7). The ground opened its mouth to receive the shed blood of Abel, and that blood now was crying out to God.

After Adam's sin, the ground was cursed. After Cain's sin, God pronounced a curse on Cain himself. This curse would have at least three consequences: (1) The ground would no longer provide him a crop. He had defiled the ground with his brother's blood. As a farmer, this was a devastating judgment. (2) Unable to settle on his land, Cain was doomed to become a fugitive and a vagabond on the earth. (3) Worst of all, Cain was separated from God (see 4:14, 16).

5. Punishment (4:13–16)

13 And Cain said unto the LORD, My punishment is greater than I can bear.

14 Behold, thou hast driven me out this day from the face of the earth, and from thy face shall I be hid; and I shall be a fugitive and a vagabond in the earth; and it shall come to pass, that every one that findeth me shall slay me.

15 And the LORD said unto him, Therefore whosoever slayeth Cain, vengeance shall be taken on him sevenfold. And the LORD set a mark upon Cain, lest any finding him should kill him.

16 And Cain went out from the presence of the LORD, and dwelt in the land of Nod, on the east of Eden.

The worst consequence of Cain's sin was that his brother was dead. The worse consequence of Cain's sin for Cain himself was his separation from God. His anger had already done that, but God had offered to receive Cain if he turned from his anger. Instead he allowed his anger to lead to murder. This act against his brother separated him from God.

Cain had tried to act as if his brother's welfare was none of his concern. God considers our relation with others as inseparably connected with our relation to God. Thus, Cain realized that his sin caused his face to be hid from God. And verse 16 says that "Cain went out from the presence of the LORD."

Cain's earlier attempt at deception and unconcern now gave way to deep concern about his own welfare. Nothing suggests any real remorse about his terrible sin. Instead he was concerned because his own punishment seemed too great to endure. He repeated God's pronouncement of condemnation from verse 12, and he added his concern about his status as a guilty fugitive. He was afraid that someone would recognize him as a murderer of his own brother and in turn kill Cain as an act of retribution.

The Lord showed as much mercy toward an unrepentant sinner as He could. He placed a mark on Cain. We are not told what it was, but the mark was designed to place Cain's life under God's protection. God vowed sevenfold vengeance on any one who presumed to play God and punish Cain. This verse underscores the consistent biblical teaching that vengeance is to be left in God's hands; no individual is to take the law into his own hands (Rom. 12:19). Later, of course, God authorized communities to establish governments to maintain order and to punish criminals (Gen. 9:5–6; Rom. 13:1–4). However, no individual has the right to take personal vengeance.

II. Cain's Descendants (Gen. 4:17–24)

Verses 17–24 provide a thumbnail sketch of human society without God. On one hand, progress was made in several areas, including musical instruments and metalwork (4:17–22). On the other hand, sin became worse with the passing generations. Lamech's callous disregard for human life went far beyond Cain's (4:25–26).

III. Birth of Seth (Gen. 4:25–26)

Chapter 4 is silent about the reaction of Adam and Eve to one of their sons being murdered by the other. They lost both their sons. One was dead. The other had to flee. Then Eve gave birth to another son, Seth. Eve said, "God . . . hath appointed me another seed instead of Abel, whom Cain slew" (4:25). After Seth had a son, Enos, "then began men to call upon the name of the LORD" (4:26). As Abel had been a man of faith, so the line of faith continued through Seth and Enos. Chapter 5 lists the names of those in this line.

SUMMARY OF BIBLE TRUTHS

1. Because life is a divine gift, murder is a terrible sin.
2. In order for worship to be acceptable to God, the worshiper's heart must be right with God and others.
3. Anger is like a dangerous wild animal in the human heart.
4. People are responsible to God for the welfare of others.
5. Sin bears the seeds of its own punishment.
6. Taking personal vengeance is a sin against God.

APPLYING THE BIBLE

1. The value of a brother. A Christian minister, a Father Bodelschwingh, "once received a visit from a government minister. . . . Unconcerned, he took this important visitor by the arm and conducted him on a tour. Suddenly Bodelschwingh recognized one of his (Christian) brethren on the opposite side of the street. Hurrying to him, he threw his arms around him. After talking to him briefly, Father Bodelschwingh returned to the government minister and tried again to take him by the arm. 'Mr. Pastor,' said the startled minister, 'Do you know for sure that this strange man has no lice?' Thereupon Bodelschwingh replied, 'Mr. Minister, one louse from the coat of this brother is worth more in God's eyes than the medal on your chest.'"[1] Tragedy broke out on earth one day because Abel did not have that kind of brother. Everybody needs a brother like that, either in the flesh or the faith or both.

2. Hatred is self-destructive. "Aristotle long ago declared that men are angry for the wrong reasons, with the wrong people, in the wrong way, and for too long a time. Even if such exhibitions of ungodly anger did not dishonor God and work havoc in the hearts of people nearby, such lack of self-control would do untold harm to one's own soul."[2]

3. Leave vengeance up to God. Perhaps Cain's problem was that Abel, in some way unknown to us, sinned against him, and he was getting back at his brother for that wrong. And perhaps, like many modern men, he felt he had to do that because somebody had to take revenge on Abel for his sin. God tells us: "Dearly beloved, avenge not yourselves, but rather give place unto wrath: for it is written, Vengeance is mine; I will repay, saith the Lord." (Rom. 12:19; see Deut. 32:35). Discuss these questions:

- Is anybody "getting by" with his sin?
- Is it possible for any one of us to exact revenge perfectly? Why?
- Can we trust God to take revenge?
- Is there any chance He won't?
- Will He make any mistake in the process?

4. Sin and Worship. Among other reasons, Cain's worship was not accepted because of his sin. Sin destroys worship; the two are incompatible. James says this about how we use our tongues: "Therewith bless we God, even the Father; and therewith curse we men, which are made after the similitude of God" (James 3:9). A terrific inconsistency! How much more murder, and then the attempt to worship!

5. Does the "amen" stick in your throat? In a striking scene, Shakespeare has Macbeth hear a prayer but, because of a sin like Cain's—that of murder—he couldn't receive the blessing of the prayer. After murdering Duncan, he hears a prayer of a servant (who with his fellowservant were awakened in the night) who prays, "God, bless us." When the second servant adds his *Amen,* Macbeth finds he cannot enter into the blessing of the prayer; he cannot utter the word "Amen." He says to his wife, "I had most need of blessing, and 'Amen' stuck in my throat." But of course it did! Is there some disobedience to God in your life, just now, that comes to mind that makes the "Amen" stick in your throat?

6. "Am I my brother's keeper?" Before you accept a glib answer, consider the information I saw recently. It was a table on the rate of illegitimacy in ten major U. S. cities for 1991. Here are the top five: Detroit, 71.0 percent (that means that 71 out of every 100 children born in Detroit were illegitimate!), Washington, D. C., 66.3 percent, St. Louis, 65.7 percent, Newark, N. J., 64.7 percent, and Atlanta, 64.4 percent.[3] Obviously, the American who thinks he can ignore those facts and escape into his enclave of sanity and sobriety and safety (not to mention substance!)is in for a rude shock. We are brothers, and we brothers had better begin to act like it!

7. Infecting others. "Thomas Carlyle tells us of an Irish widow who in Edinburgh with three helpless children sought help in vain, fell ill of typhus, and infecting seventeen others, died. 'The forlorn Irish widow,' cries Carlyle grimly, 'applies to her fellow creatures,' 'Behold I am sinking bare of help. I am your sister; one God made us. You must help me.' They answered, 'No, impossible; thou art no sister of ours!' But she proves her sisterhood; her typhus kills THEM; they actually were her brothers, though denying it." The author later adds, "No one is safe till all are safe. No privilege is secure till all possess it. No blessing is really owned until it universally is shared. That service to 'one of the least of these my brethren,' so far from being a superfluous ideal, is an ineradicable law of life, is indicated by this basic fact: in the last analysis self-preservation depends upon it."[4]

8. For discussion. Cain's anger manifested itself in a devastating way. Perhaps that explains why Jesus used such strong language about hate (see Matt. 5:21–24, 43–48; 19:15–17). Discuss these questions:

▶ Why was Cain so angry with Abel?

▶ Could their problem have been solved and the relationship saved? How?

▶ What if Cain and Abel had applied Jesus' problem-solving process stated in Matthew 18:15–17?

▶ How does the story of Cain and Abel prove the lie of people who say, "It's nobody else's business what happens between us? Nobody else is involved."

TEACHING THE BIBLE

▶ *Main Idea:* Cain and Abel's experience shows the consequences of sin.

▶ *Suggested Teaching Aim:* To lead adults to see that all sin has consequences.

A TEACHING OUTLINE

Consequences of Sin
1. *The Gift of Life (4:1–2)*
2. *Acceptable and Unacceptable Worship (4:3–5)*
3. *Anger and Murder (4:6–8)*
4. *Condemnation (4:9–12)*
5. *Punishment (4:13–16)*

Introduce the Bible Study
IN ADVANCE, arrange chairs in two sections, one marked *Cain* and the other marked *Abel.* Place a sheet of paper and a pencil in each chair. Place a large poster on the wall with these words on it: *Who? What? When? Where? How? Why?* Ask those sitting in each section to listen for answers to these questions. Also, ask them to listen for principles that would apply today.

Search for Biblical Truth
Ask a volunteer to read aloud Genesis 4:1–2. Lecture briefly describing (1) Eve's two sons; (2) how the sons earned their living.

DISCUSS: If all children are a gift from God, why are some so abused and ill treated? (How we respond to God's gifts is up to us.)

Ask a volunteer to read aloud 4:3–5. Lecture briefly to explain the three possible explanations of God's displeasure with Cain's offering and acceptance of Abel's (see "Studying the Bible").

DISCUSS: Does God ever reject any of our gifts that we give today? How do we know?

Ask a volunteer to read aloud 4:6–8. Lecture briefly to explain: (1) God's questioning Cain about his anger; (2) God's warning Cain about the consequences of his anger.

DISCUSS: How do we feed our anger and what are the results in family situations today?

Ask a volunteer to read aloud 4:9. Lecture briefly to explain: (1) Why God asked Cain about Abel; (2) Cain's refusal to accept his responsibility for treating Abel as a brother.

DISCUSS: How are we our brothers' and sisters' keepers?

Ask a volunteer to read aloud 4:10–12. Lecture briefly to explain: (1) how sin carries the seeds of condemnation; (2) The three consequences of God's curse: (a) The ground would no longer provide him a crop; (b) Cain was doomed to become a fugitive and a vagabond; (c) Cain separated himself from God.

DISCUSS: Does all sin have consequences? Explain.

Ask a volunteer to read 4:13–16. Lecture briefly to explain Cain's reaction to his punishment.

DISCUSS: What is the relationship between worshiping God and treating others properly?

Call for groups to share their summaries of Cain and Abel.

Read aloud the six "Summary of Bible Truths" to summarize the lesson. Ask members to write a guideline based on each statement for proper behavior in families.

Give the Truth a Personal Focus

Ask, Can we ever get away with any sin? How do we suffer consequences? Why, then, do we continue to try to get away with sin? What can we do with our sin?

Close in prayer that all will confess their sin and ask God for forgiveness.

---

1. Quoted in Carl F. H. Henry and Stanley Mooneyham, eds., *One Race, One Gospel, One Task* (Minneapolis: World-Wide Publications, 1967), 1:93–94.

2. Andrew Blackwood, *The Growing Minister* (Nashville: Abingdon Press, 1960), 109.

3. Quoted in William Bennett, *The Index of Leading Cultural Indicators* (New York: Simon & Schuster, 1994), 48.

4. Harry Emerson Fosdick, *The Meaning of Service* (London: SCM, 1921), 56–57.

Judgment and New Beginning

Background Passage: Genesis 6:5–9:17
Focal Passages: Genesis 6:5–8; 7:1–4; 9:12–17

The great flood in Noah's time is one of the most significant events of the initial period of Old Testament history: the period of the beginnings. Genesis 6:5–9:17 contains some of the foundational teachings about sin, punishment, God's grief over sin, God's grace, deliverance, and hope.

▶**Study Aim:** *To identify basic biblical teachings about sin, punishment, grace, deliverance, and hope.*

STUDYING THE BIBLE

OUTLINE AND SUMMARY

    I. **Judgment (Gen. 6:5–7:24)**
        1. Total depravity (6:5)
        2. God's grief (6:6–7)
        3. God's grace (6:8–9)
        4. Preparations for the flood (6:10–7:9)
        5. The flood (7:10–24)
    II. **A New Beginning (Gen. 8:1–9:17)**
        1. Building an altar (8:1–22)
        2. God's covenant with Noah (9:1–17)

Sinful humanity became totally corrupt in every way (6:5). God was sorry about what they had done to His good creation, and He was grieved by their sin (6:6–7). Noah, who walked with God, found grace in God's eyes (6:8–9). Noah obeyed God's instructions about preparing for the flood by building an ark (6:10–7:9). The flood destroyed all life on earth except for the people and creatures on the ark (7:10–24). After they emerged from the ark on dry ground, Noah built an altar and offered sacrifices to God (8:1–22). God made an unconditional covenant with Noah and all later generations: He gave the rainbow as a sign that He never again would destroy the earth by water (9:1–17).

I. Judgment (Gen. 6:5–7:24)

1. Total depravity (6:5)

5 And God saw that the wickedness of man was great in the earth, and that every imagination of the thoughts of his heart was only evil continually.

Compare the words "God saw" in this verse with its repetition throughout Genesis 1. In chapter 1, God looked at His creative work and "saw that it was good" (1:10, 12, 18, 20) or "very good" (1:31). In Genesis 6:5, God saw how His good creation had been corrupted by human sin.

Verse 5 describes the end result of the sin of Adam and Eve. Their sin became worse when Cain murdered his own brother (Gen. 4:1–16). As the line of Cain continued through the early centuries, they became worse and worse (Gen. 4:17–24). Verse 5 describes the final state of a person or society that gives itself totally to sin.

Verse 5 is one of the strongest Bible statements about total depravity, the end result of unchecked sin. The verse spares no words to describe the depth of human wickedness. "Wickedness" translates a word that describes a state of evil, not just sinful acts. This evil state of humans was "great." "Imagination of the thoughts of the heart" refers to the intention and purpose of human thoughts and actions. Notice the all-inclusive words "every . . . only . . . continually." Genesis 6:11 adds, "The earth also was corrupt before God, and the earth was filled with violence." Genesis 8:21 adds of each sinner, "The imagination of man's heart is evil from his youth."

This is the ultimate description of total depravity. Not all sinners hit rock bottom as they did. Total depravity, therefore, can refer to the universal sin in every life—the sin of something twisted and wrong at the core of the human heart. Our best efforts to live without God are doomed to fail because of the reality of human sin.

2. God's grief (6:6–7)

> **6 And it repented the LORD that he had made man on the earth, and it grieved him at his heart.**
>
> **7 And the LORD said, I will destroy man whom I have created from the face of the earth; both man, and beast, and the creeping thing, and the fowls of the air; for it repenteth me that I have made them.**

The word translated "repented" needs to be interpreted in light of the word *grieved*. In the human sense of repenting, God "is not a man that he should repent" (1 Sam. 15:29). That is, God is never sorry for something wrong He has done. Nor does He change His ultimate purpose. When this word is used of God, it refers to a change in God's treatment of humanity as a result of human actions. In Jonah 3:10, God repented of the judgment He had said was coming on Nineveh. He did not destroy them because they repented of their sins. In Genesis 6:6–7, the terrible sins of the people caused God to wipe them out. He did not decide that His creation had been a mistake; He announced that the sinners of that day and other land and air creatures would be wiped out.

Yet even as He announced the terrible judgment, God was "grieved." Sin not only stirs the wrath of God against sin; it grieves Him because of the evil people are doing and the sure judgment that is coming on them. This grief of God over human sin is one of the early Bible clues to the heart of the loving God who later sent His only Son to save a perishing world (John 3:16). God is not impassive and unmoved; instead He is active and caring. The ultimate revelation of the love of God is at the cross.

3. God's grace (6:8–9)

> **8 But Noah found grace in the eyes of the LORD.**

Noah was first mentioned in Genesis 5:30, at the end of the line of people of faith descended from Adam through Seth and Enos (see Gen. 4:35–36). These people, in contrast to the line of Cain, had continued to call on the name of the Lord. Enoch, for example, "walked with God" (5:24). The same words are used in Genesis 6:9 of Noah.

"Grace" means favor. God showed favor to Noah by saving him and his family from the flood. Noah was a righteous man, but his goodness came from his walk with the Lord. The New Testament revelation about God's grace is summed up in Ephesians 2:8–10.

4. Preparations for the flood (6:10–7:9)

1 And the LORD said unto Noah, Come thou and all thy house into the ark; for thee have I seen righteous before me in this generation.

2 Of every clean beast thou shalt take to thee by sevens, the male and his female: and of beasts that are not clean by two, the male and his female.

3 Of fowls also of the air by sevens, the male and the female; to keep seed alive upon the face of all the earth.

4 For yet seven days and I will cause it to rain upon the earth forty days and forty nights; and every living substance that I have made will I destroy from off the face of the earth.

God told Noah of His decision to destroy the earth (6:10–13). He explained to Noah how to build an ark because He planned to destroy the earth by water (6:14–17). God promised not only to spare Noah and his family but also to make a covenant with Noah (6:18). God told Noah to take two of each living creature to go on the ark (6:19–20). Noah also was to store plenty of food (6:20). Noah obeyed the Lord's instructions (6:22).

At the time appointed by God, He told Noah and his family to enter the ark. The word *come* in this context is more than just a command to enter an ark; it is an example of an invitation to deliverance from death unto life. Thus it has this in common with later Bible uses of the word *come* (Isa. 1:18; 55:1; Matt. 12:28; Rev. 22:17).

Seven of each kind of clean animal were to be spared. The reason given in verse 3 is "to keep seed alive upon the face of all the earth." Later after the ark landed safely on dry ground, some of the clean animals were used as sacrifices (8:20). God told Noah that rain would fall continually for 40 days and nights until all living things were destroyed. Noah obeyed the Lord (7:5–9).

5. The flood (7:10–24)

On the day appointed by God "were all the fountains of the great deep broken up, and the windows of heaven were opened" (7:11). As God had predicted, it rained forty days and nights (7:12). Earlier in the day, Noah and his family and all the animals had entered the ark, "and the LORD shut him in" (7:12–16). As the waters rose, the ark floated on the waters; but all other people, land animals, and birds perished during the 150 days of the flood (7:18–24).

II. A New Beginning (Gen. 8:1–9:17)

1. Building an altar (8:1–22)

God remembered his promise to Noah and caused the waters to begin to recede until finally the tops of mountains were visible (8:1–5). After forty days, Noah sent out a raven and a dove; but the dove returned, having found no resting place on earth (8:6–9). A week later, Noah sent out the dove again; and the bird returned with an olive leaf (8:10–11). After another week, the dove was sent out again and did not return (8:12). When Noah removed the covering of the ark, he found that the ground was dry (8:13–14). The Lord told Noah that he and his family and all the animals should leave the ark. The Lord repeated the command to be fruitful and multiply that was part of His instructions in Genesis 1 (8:15–19). Noah built an altar and offered as sacrifices each kind of clean animal and bird (8:20). God promised that he would no longer curse the ground for man's sake, and He promised that the seasons would last as long as the earth lasted (8:21–22).

2. God's covenant with Noah (9:1–17)

12 And God said, This is the token of the covenant which I make between me and you and every living creature that is with you, for perpetual generations:

13 I do set my bow in the cloud, and it shall be for a token of a covenant between me and the earth.

14 And it shall come to pass, when I bring a cloud over the earth, that the bow shall be seen in the cloud:

15 And I will remember my covenant, which is between me and you and every living creature of all flesh; and the waters shall no more become a flood to destroy all flesh.

16 And the bow shall be in the cloud; and I will look upon it, that I may remember the everlasting covenant between God and every living creature of all flesh that is upon the earth.

17 And God said unto Noah, This is the token of the covenant, which I have established between me and all flesh that is upon the earth.

When Noah and his family emerged from the ark, God made a new beginning for them and for other creatures on earth. The basic truth here appears many times throughout the Bible: Beyond judgment, God offers hope and a new beginning.

This new beginning was in the form of a covenant. The Bible speaks of several covenants. Later God made a covenant with Abraham (Gen. 17); He made a covenant with Israel at Mount Sinai (Exod. 19); and in Jesus Christ, God offers a new covenant.

Several features of the covenant with Noah are brought out in verses 12–17. Some of them are repeated several times. (1) The covenant took the form of an unconditional promise by God that He would never again destroy the entire earth by water (9:15). The New Testament, however, reminds us that the earth will be destroyed by fire; but it also promises a new heaven and a new earth (2 Pet. 3:3–13). (2) The promise was made not only with Noah but also with all the other creatures and with all future generations. "Perpetual generations" is mentioned in verse 12. Some words describing every living creature are repeated in nearly every verse in the passage. (3) The rainbow was given as a sign of the promise that God would remember and honor this covenant (9:13, 14, 16).

SUMMARY OF BIBLE TRUTHS

1. Sin gets worse and worse.
2. Continual sin and refusal to repent eventually brings judgment.
3. Sin grieves the heart of God.
4. God offers grace to those who walk with Him.
5. God delivers those who trust and obey.
6. God offers a new beginning to those who trust and obey Him.

APPLYING THE BIBLE

1. Seeing the truth. An antique dealer found a secret compartment in a chest of drawers. When he opened it, a set of spectacles dropped out. Over the rim of the spectacles was inscribed *veritas,* the Latin word for "truth." The man put the glasses on and, much to his surprise, found that he could see into the very heart of things, could peer through the facades and shams and cosmetics into the true nature of reality. He had all sorts of fun looking at things, not as they appeared, but as they really were. In the final scene of this strange story, told by Alfred Hitchcock, the man puts the glasses on one night and looks into the mirror and falls dead, stricken by the horror of what he sees inside his own heart. Now let's ask ourselves, "Are people really all that bad?" That is a very crucial question, and one that we must answer properly in order to understand our world.

2. Quick Quotes.

‣ "If there are so many conflicts today, it is because of what Weidle has called 'the great insurrection of man against God, which is the essence of modern history" (Paul Tournier).[1]

‣ "There is only one empirically verifiable doctrine of theology—original sin" (George Bernard Shaw).

‣ "There must be a vein of original sin in humanity everywhere to which Hitlerism makes a strong appeal. The moral is that civilization is nowhere and never secure. It is a thin cake of custom overlaying a molten mass of wickedness that is always boiling up for an opportunity to burst out."[2]

‣ "Nature has left this tincture in the blood/That all men would be tyrants if they could" (Daniel Defoe, "The Kentish Petition").

‣ "It is essential not to have faith in human nature. Such faith is a recent heresy and a very disastrous one" (Herbert Butterfield).[3]

3. The thin veneer of civilization. William Golding wrote, in 1954, his novel *Lord of the Flies,* which some see as a parable of the entire human experience. He portrays a group of English choirboys stranded on a tropical island and has them quickly revert to the life of proud, self-centered savages who not only harass and bully each other, but are perfectly willing to resort to murder to get their way. The last scene of the story has them standing on the shore of the island, having ravaged each other and the island itself. Human nature, left to itself, always comes to the same place.

4. God's calendar. God will judge all sin. The Latin word *kalendae,* from which we get our English word *calendar,* referred to a time in Roman society when accounts became due. We need to look, not only at the calendars of the world, but the calendar of eternity, not at our own calendars only, but God's.

5. Too smart for his own good. The local papers carried an Associated Press article entitled, "'Perfect Crime' may send genius to electric chair." It is the story of a member of MENSA, the club for persons with a high IQ. Prosecutors said this genius had accomplished the almost-perfect crime. Due to a small detail, however, he was caught, tried, and now faces possible death in the electric chair.[4]

6. The mills of God. In his poem "Retribution," Henry Wadsworth Longfellow wrote these familiar lines:

> "Though the mills of God grind slowly,
> yet they grind exceeding small;
> Though with patience He stands waiting,
> with exactness grinds He all."

7. Self-deception. A Chinese story tells of a man who stole a clock one night. While the thief was carrying it off to hide it, the clock began to chime. The man solved the problem by putting cotton in his ears.

8. Beginning again. An unknown poet wrote:

> I wish there were some wonderful place-
> Called the land of beginning again;
> Where all of our mistakes and all our heartaches'
> And all of our selfish grief
> Could be dumped like a shabby old coat at the door
> And never be put on again.

There is such a place, and it is the cross of Jesus! "But where sin abounded, grace did much more abound" (Rom. 5:20).

9. God's will for us. In our study for the day, we have noticed that Noah "walked with God." God's plan is for us (a) to recognize, confess, and repent of our sin, (b) to come to Christ in faith for salvation, and (c) to walk with God. An old hymn puts it powerfully and truthfully:

> Trust and obey, for there's no other way
> To be happy in Jesus, but to trust and obey."

10. For discussion:
▶ Is our society any better morally today than Noah's society?
▶ Does God enjoy punishing us for our sin?
▶ Why didn't God make it impossible for us to sin? Would you have wanted such a situation? Why?

> What goes wrong if we trust God but do not obey Him? If we attempt to obey Him but do not trust Him?

TEACHING THE BIBLE

> *Main Idea:* God offers judgment and a new beginning when we sin.
> *Suggested Teaching Aim:* To lead adults to accept God's judgment and new beginning for their sin.

A TEACHING OUTLINE

Judgment and New Beginning

1. *Judgment (Gen. 6:5–7:24)*
2. *A New Beginning (Gen. 8:1–9:17)*

Introduce the Bible Study

Use illustration #1 from "Applying the Bible" to introduce the lesson. Read the Main Idea.

Search for Biblical Truth

IN ADVANCE, number and write out the seven statements in "Outline and Summary" on small strips of paper and give to seven persons to read when you call on them. Ask the person with the first statement to read it at this time. Ask members to look at Genesis 6:5 in their Bibles. Ask: Do you remember an earlier time when the phrase "God saw" was used? (Gen. 1:10, 12, 18, 20, 31.) How is verse 5 related to Adam and Eve's sin? (Describes end result of their sin.) On a chalkboard or a large sheet of paper write the following (omit the italicized words):

The Human Situation	
Its Condition:	*wickedness, evil*
Its State:	*great*
Its Inclusiveness:	*every, only, continually*

Ask members to read verse 5 and select words from the text that describe these three aspects of the human situation.

Ask members to look at 6:6–7. Ask the person with the second summary statement to read it. Ask, What was God's reaction to this human situation? (Grieved.) Define "repent" as referring "to a change in God's treatment of humanity as a result of human actions." Ask, What act of history proves God's great grief and concern for human sin? (The cross.)

Ask members to look at 6:8. Call for the third summary statement to be read. Ask, What set Noah apart from the rest of the world at that time? (Found grace.) Why do you think Noah found grace in God's sight? (Because of the way he lived.)

Ask members to look at 7:1–4. Ask the person with the fourth summary statement to read it. Ask: What was God's invitation to Noah? (Come.) Can you think of some other uses of the word *come* that extend

God's invitation? (Among others: Isa. 1:18; 55:1; Matt. 12:28; Rev. 22:17.) How many of each kind of animal did Noah take on the ark? (Two of unclean; seven of clean.)

Ask the persons with the fifth, sixth, and seventh summary statements to read them. Ask members to look at 9:12–17. Ask: What was the significance of the rainbow? Why do you think God would give the human race a second chance? What were the features of the covenant God made with Noah? (Unconditional promise not to destroy the world by water; promise made with future generations; rainbow was sign of the covenant.)

Read the following six statements and ask members if they agree or disagree and why. Then ask the follow-up questions.

1. Sin gets worse and worse. Are our sins as individuals worse now than in Noah's time?
2. Continual sin and refusal to repent eventually bring judgment. How does God bring about His judgment on us individually? as a nation?
3. Sin grieves the heart of God. What sins have you committed that grieved God? (All of them.)
4. God offers grace to those who walk with Him. What do you need to do to receive God's offered grace?
5. God delivers those who trust and obey. Why do we find it so hard to trust and obey God?
6. God offers a new beginning to those who trust and obey. What do you need to do to trust and obey God so you can begin anew?

Give the Truth a Personal Focus

Use illustration #4 from "Applying the Bible" to encourage members to trust and obey God and to begin a new walk with Him. Close in prayer.

---

1. Paul Tournier, Escape from Loneliness (Philadelphia: Westminster Press, 1962), 149.
2. Arnold Toynbee, quoted in Vance Havner, In Times Like These (New York: Revell, 1969), 62.
3. Herbert Butterfield, Christianity and History (London: Fontana Books, 1964), 66.
4. Reported in St. Petersburg Times, 2/10/1991, p. 4b.

God's Call to Abram

Background Passage: Genesis 11:27–12:9
Focal Passage: Genesis 11:31–12:9

Abraham marks another new beginning in the Book of Genesis (Beginnings). The first beginning was with Adam and Eve, but sin became so bad that the flood came. The second beginning was with Noah, but sinful humanity tried to erect the tower of Babel and brought the judgment of being scattered (11:1–9). God then made a different kind of new beginning. He chose Abraham and his descendants to become a channel of blessing to all nations.

▶**Study Aim:** *To identify God's commands and blessings to Abraham and evidences of Abraham's faith in God.*

STUDYING THE BIBLE

OUTLINE AND SUMMARY
  I.   **Abram's Heritage (Gen. 11:27–32)**
  II. **God's Commands and Promises (Gen. 12:1–3)**
       1. **Commands (12:1)**
       2. **Promises (12:2–3)**
  III. **Abram's Responses (Gen. 12:4–9)**
       1. **Obedient faith (12:4–5)**
       2. **Pilgrim faith (12:6–9)**

Abram traveled from Ur to Haran with his father Terah; and after Terah died, Abram headed for Canaan (11:27–32). God commanded Abram to leave his country and family and go to a land the Lord would show him (12:1). The Lord promised to bless Abram and to make him a channel of blessing to all nations (12:2–3). Abram obeyed God and went to Canaan (12:4–5). He lived in Canaan; and as he moved about, he built altars and worshiped the Lord (12:6–9).

I. Abram's Heritage (Gen. 11:27–32)

31 And Terah took Abram his son, and Lot the son of Haran his son's son, and Sarai his daughter in law, his son Abram's wife; and they went forth with them from Ur of the Chaldees, to go into the land of Canaan; and they came unto Haran, and dwelt there.

32 And the days of Terah were two hundred and five years: and Terah died in Haran.

Terah took Abram, Sarai, and Lot (Haran's son) with him and left Ur. His destination was Canaan, but he stopped at Haran. Terah settled and later died there. Ur was an old city in the time of Abram. In traveling from Ur to Canaan, Terah and his family would have traveled around the so-called Fertile Crescent—a crescent-shaped area of fertility that went north of the desert. Haran was at the western end of the crescent. Canaan was farther south.

In light of God's call to Abram in Genesis 12:1, several questions arise about Terah: Why did he leave Ur? Why did he settle in Haran and never go on to Canaan? A possible answer to the first question is that Abram was the one who heard the call to go to Canaan, and Terah decided to go with him. A possible answer to the second question is that Terah never felt the strong call to go to Canaan that Abram felt. Perhaps he even wanted to deter Abram from leaving him and the rest of the family.

Ur was a center of moon worship. In fact, Joshua 24:2 implies that Terah had partaken in this pagan worship. If so, he may have tried to combine such worship with faith in the Lord. Abram, on the other hand, seems to have had a purer faith in the Lord alone. This raises another question: Why did Abram stay so long in Haran if God had called him to leave his family and go to Canaan? Abram probably was acting out of loyalty to his old father.

II. God's Commands and Promises (Gen. 12:1–3)
1. Commands (12:1)

1 Now the LORD had said unto Abram, Get thee out of thy country, and from thy kindred, and from thy father's house, unto a land that I will shew thee.

Did Abram hear this call in Ur, in Haran, or in both? Stephen said that the call came before he went to Haran (Acts 7:2; see also Gen. 15:7; Neh. 9:7). Some Bible students think that God originally called Abram in Ur and later renewed the call in Haran. The commands of God were for Abram to leave his country, his kin, and his father's family and to travel to a land that the Lord would show him. The threefold leaving would surely apply to leaving Ur, but it also would fit Haran. His family had settled in Haran. Years later when Abraham was seeking a wife for Isaac, he sent his servant to Haran to the family of his brother Nahor (Gen. 24).

Genesis 11:31 mentions Canaan as the destination, but 12:1 does not name the place. At some point, Abram learned that the destination was Canaan; however, when the call first came, God called on him to go forth to a destination known only to God. Here we see the faith and obedience of Abram. He was asked to leave his country and family—sources of security in the ancient world. And he was commanded to set forth on a journey without knowing where God was leading him. "By faith Abraham, when he was called to go out into a place which he should after receive as an inheritance, obeyed; and he went out, not knowing whither he went" (Heb. 11:8).

2. Promises (12:2–3)

2 And I will make of thee a great nation, and I will bless thee, and make thy name great; and thou shalt be a blessing:
3 And I will bless them that bless thee, and curse him that curseth thee: and in thee shall all families of the earth be blessed.

The key words in this sevenfold promise are some form of "bless." God promised to make of Abram a great nation. As later chapters unfold the story, this became a real test of Abram's faith. His wife was barren, and they were both getting older each year. The rest of the Old Testament shows how crucial this nation of chosen people became in the history of God's plan of redemption.

The promises to bless Abram and make his name great were also promises to the great nation of his descendants. These words are set over against the sinful goal of those who built the tower of Babel. They said, "Let us build us a city and a tower, whose top may reach unto heaven; and let us make us a name" (Gen. 11:4). They were trying to become great by building a brave new world without God; God promised that only people of faith in the great God would know true greatness.

Some scholars insist that "thou shalt be a blessing" is actually an imperative. If so, it should read, "Be thou a blessing." God was promising to bless Abraham and also calling him to be a channel of blessings. One of the main mistakes of the Old Testament chosen people was to see their choice only as a privilege, not also as a responsibility. God blesses us in order that we in turn might be a blessing to others.

The response of other nations and people to Abraham and his descendants would determine whether the others received God's blessing or curse. Ultimately, the New Testament says that the true seed of Abraham was Jesus Christ (Gal. 3:14–16). People's response to this seed of Abraham determines whether they receive eternal life or everlasting condemnation.

The last of the seven blessings is crucial for the rest of biblical revelation. God promised Abram, "In thee shall all the nations of the earth be blessed." The Old Testament chosen people of Israel were called to be different from other nations, but they were to be different in order that they might be able to bear witness to other nations. Throughout their early history, their problem was that they compromised their distinctive faith and way of life and thus became like pagan nations. After the exile and into the first century, many of them went to the other extreme. They kept their distinctive faith and way of life, but they regarded Gentiles as dogs.

This issue was the hottest debate among the first Jewish believers in Jesus as Israel's Messiah. Many wanted Him to be just for Jews and for those Gentiles who would become Jews. Others, like Paul, insisted that God's purpose had always been to use Israel to provide the way of salvation for all nations. Paul quoted Genesis 12:3 as one of the key passages supporting this view (Gal. 3:8).

III. Abram's Responses (Gen. 12:4–9)
1. Obedient faith (12:4–5)

4 So Abram departed, as the LORD had spoken unto him; and Lot went with him: and Abram was seventy and five years old when he departed out of Haran.

5 And Abram took Sarai his wife, and Lot his brother's son, and all their substance that they had gathered, and the souls that they had gotten in Haran; and they went forth to go into the land of Canaan; and into the land of Canaan they came.

We have no record of what Abram said, but we do have a record of what he did. He and his company "departed" or "went forth." At some point, the Lord had revealed to him that he was to go to the land of Canaan, "and into the land of Canaan they came." Abram responded to God's call by obeying. Real faith is always seen in actions.

Abram's age is mentioned here and at several later places in the biblical record. One purpose of this was to show how he and Sarai continued to age, each year making the birth of the child of promise more unlikely by human standards (16:6; 17:1, 24; 21:5).

Abram took with him his wife and his nephew Lot. Lot is something of an enigma. We are not told why Lot went. The most likely explanation is that Abraham felt obligated to help his dead brother's son. Later events would test Abram's love for his nephew (Gen. 13–14; 18–19). Abram also took all their accumulated possessions and "the souls they had gotten in Haran." These were probably servants, since Abram had many servants (Gen. 14:14).

2. Pilgrim faith (12:6–9)

6 And Abram passed through the land unto the place of Sichem, unto the plain of Moreh. And the Canaanite was then in the land.

7 And the LORD appeared unto Abram, and said, Unto thy seed will I give this land: and there builded he an altar unto the LORD, who appeared unto him.

8 And he removed from thence unto a mountain on the east of Bethel, and pitched his tent, having Bethel on the west, and Hai on the east: and there he builded an altar unto the LORD, and called upon the name of the LORD.

9 And Abram journeyed, going on still toward the south.

Shortly after Abram arrived in Canaan, the Lord promised to give the land to his descendants. This is the first explicit promise of the land, although the idea is implicit in God's promises in 12:2–3. The promise of the land was made many times to Abram's descendants, until they finally went into Canaan under Joshua. Yet at the very time when the Lord was promising to give the land to Abram, the land was already inhabited and belonged to the Canaanites. Abram did not find an empty land, nor did he find a warm welcome from those who lived there. As far as we know, Abram never legally owned any of the land except the burial area for his family (Gen. 23).

This was probably one reason that Abram did so much traveling when he arrived in Canaan. He was looking for a place where he could pitch his tents without encountering strong opposition. Therefore, he went to such places as Shechem, Bethel, Hai, and the south (Negeb). Eventually, he seems to have settled around Hebron and Mamre (13:8; 18:1).

Hebrews 11:13–16 describes this aspect of Abram's faith as pilgrim faith. He lived in a land that God had promised to his descendants; yet he himself was a stranger (foreigner) and a pilgrim. Abram dared to believe that God would keep His promises to him and his descendants. He lived by faith in the word of the unseen God whose promises were as yet unfulfilled. The Canaanites had gods that they could see, and they already had what they considered fulfilled fruits of their religious practices. What did Abram have? He had only the word of a God who allowed no images to be made of Him, and His bright promises were yet to be fulfilled.

Another aspect of pilgrim faith is that it is a mobile faith. It is not tied to one land, location, or building. Thus, wherever Abram went, he built an altar and worshiped God.

SUMMARY OF BIBLE TRUTHS

1. God calls His people to trust His promises and to obey His commands.
2. God's people are blessed in order to bless others.
3. God's plan is universal in scope.
4. True faith is seen in actions.
5. Pilgrim faith is trusting the word of the unseen God to fulfill His yet unfulfilled promises.
6. A person of true faith worships God wherever he moves.

APPLYING THE BIBLE

1. Faith in action. I grew up in a rural community in which one of the most-often told stories was about a man whose mule died. Other farmers expressed their condolences, but one man said it this way: "Jim, I'm sorry your mule died. In fact, I'm sorry ten dollars worth." And with that, he handed the mule-less farmer a ten-dollar bill.

2. A test of faith. Blondin was a famous tightrope walker of the last century. He once strung a rope across Niagara Falls and asked the crowd how many thought he could walk across the falls. When they shouted "We believe! We believe!" he asked which one of them would be the lucky person to be carried across on his back. The crowd fell silent.[1]

3. Columbus and his trip. Somebody once said that if you are puzzled about following the Lord, remember that, when Columbus left Spain, he didn't know where he was going; when he arrived, he didn't know where he was; and when he returned he didn't know where he had been.

4. Involved but not committed! Did you hear about the kamikaze pilot who flew sixteen missions without incident? That represents involvement without commitment! "Faith" without works!

5. The man who never died. A poet has it this way:

> There was a very cautious man
> who never laughed or cried
> He never risked, he never lost,
> he never won nor tried.
> And when one day he passed away
> his insurance was denied,
> for since he never really lived
> they claimed he never died.[2]

6. Generous with others' money. Teofilo ("friend of God") said to a new Christian Christobel ("Christbearer"), "If you had a hundred sheep, would you give fifty of them for the Lord's work?" When his friend said he would, he asked a second question: "Would you do the same with a hundred cows?" Again, when Christobel said he would, a third question was posed: "Would you do the same if you had a hundred horses?" "Yes," said the new Christian. Then, "If you had two pigs, would you give one of them to Him?" The sobered Christobel said, "No, I wouldn't; and you have no right to ask me, Teofilo, for you know I have two pigs."[3]

7. Faith expressed. Study Mary's great expression of faith in her response to the angelic annunciation of the birth of Jesus (Luke 1:26–38). Then compare her expression of faith with Abraham's. Then discuss these two, comparing and contrasting them.

In his study of trust (or faith), Dr. Julian Rotter from the University of Connecticut found that, contrary to popular opinion,

▶ Trusting persons tend to be less gullible than non-trusting people;

▶ Trusting persons tend to have a higher IQ then sceptical people;

▶ Trusting persons live happier lives than non-trusting persons;

▶ Trusting persons tend to be more trustworthy than non-trusting people; and

▶ Trusting persons are less likely to fall for the con artist.[4]

8. Taking action. In *The Screwtape Letters* of C. S. Lewis, the devil Screwtape tells a young tempter how to treat a new Christian: "The great thing is to prevent his doing anything. As long as he does not convert it into action, it does not matter how much he thinks about this new repentance. Let the little brute wallow in it. Let him, if he has any bent that way, write a book about it; that is often an excellent way of sterilizing the seeds which the Enemy plants in a human soul. Let him do anything but act. No amount of piety in his imagination and affections will harm us if we can keep it out of his will. As one of the humans has said, active habits are strengthened by repitition but passive ones are weakened. The more often he feels without acting, the less he will be able ever to act, and, in the long run, the less he will be able to feel."[5] Discuss these questions:

▶ Has the plan of the "Enemy" worked for many Christians?

▶ Describe the process behind the principle stated in the last sentence of the preceding paragraph.

▶ Did Abraham's faith grow or diminish because of his obedience? Is that a general rule?

▶ Name some things Abraham had to leave to express his faith? I heard a man say some time ago that, typically, to follow God, we must leave people, places, practices, pleasures, and philosophies. Was that true of Abraham?

▶ Compare God's command to Abraham with Jesus' command to His disciples: "If any man will come after me, let him deny himself, and take up his cross, and follow me" (Matt. 16:24)? How do these differ, if at all?

TEACHING THE BIBLE

▶ *Main Idea:* God calls people to His service.
▶ *Suggested Teaching Aim:* To lead adults to respond to God's call for their lives.

A TEACHING OUTLINE

God's Call to Abram (Gen. 11:27–12:9)

1. *Abram's Heritage (11:27–32)*
2. *God's Commands and Promises (12:1–3)*
3. *Abram's Responses (12:4–9)*

Introduce the Bible Study

On a chalkboard or a large sheet of paper write:

Beginnings

God's Plan	Human Response	God's Response
Adam and Eve	Sin	Era ended in the flood
Noah	Sin	Era ended in the tower of Babel
Abraham	Sin	Era ended in the cross

Explain how God began something new and how each time it ended in sin.

Search for Biblical Truth

IN ADVANCE, copy the title and three points in "A Teaching Outline" on large strips of paper. Place the title and first point on the focal wall. On a map of the Old Testament world, locate Ur, Haran, and Canaan.

Read aloud Genesis 11:31–32. **IN ADVANCE,** assign a member to research Ur and Haran. Call for the report at this time. Ask, According to 12:1, what three things did God call Abram to leave? (Country, kindred, father's house.)

IN ADVANCE, write "12:2–3" on a large sheet of paper. Place the paper on the wall, and ask members to identify the sevenfold promise God made to Abram in these verses. Ask: What made the promise difficult to believe? (Abram's and Sarai's ages.) Ask members to turn to Genesis 11:4 and contrast how the people planned to make a name for themselves and how God promised Abram He would do it. Ask, How did Abraham's descendants fail to live up to the last part of the blessing ("In thee shall all the nations of the earth be blessed.")

Read aloud 12:4–5. Ask, Why did Genesis mention Abram's age at this point? (To prepare us for the great miracle God is going to perform.) Which do you think contributed most to the fact that "into the land of Canaan they came": God's faithfulness or Abram's actions?

Read aloud 12:6–9. On the map of the Old Testament, locate Moreh, Shechem (Sichem), and Bethel. Point out Hebron as the place near which Abram finally settled. Ask, What was the first thing Abram built in Canaan? (Altar.) How do you think Abram felt about the Lord promising him a land that was already occupied by Canaanites?

Ask members to list acts of faith on Abram's part at this time in his life. (Lived by faith—he had nothing tangible.)

Give the Truth a Personal Focus

Read aloud each of the statements in "Summary of Bible Truths" and suggest that these statements summarize Abram's life. Now ask: Which of these statements is not still true today? Do you believe God still calls people like Abram? What is keeping you from responding to God's call?

---

1. Benjamin P. Browne, *Tales of Baptist Daring* (Philadelphia: Judson Press, 1961), 119–23, as quoted by Jim Highfill in *Illustrating Paul's Letter to the Romans.*

2. Dennis Waitley, *Being the Best* (Nashville: Thomas Nelson, 1978), 115.

3. Walter Knight, ed., *Knight's Master Book of New Illustrations* (Grand Rapids: Eerdmans, 1956), 239.

4. Robert Schuller, *Self-Esteem: The New Reformation* (Waco: Word Books, 1982), 86.

5. C. S. Lewis, *The Screwtape Letters* (Toronto, New York, London, Sydney: Bantam Books, 1982), 39.

A Promise Fulfilled

Background Passages: Genesis 15:1–18:15; 21:1–7
Focal Passages: Genesis 15:1–6; 17:17–21; 21:1–2

Have you noticed how many great stages of divine work in the Bible begin with the birth of a baby? We think immediately of Jesus; but there were others: Isaac, Moses, Samuel, John the Baptist. None of these was born in the same unique way as Jesus, but three of them were born to women who had been barren—and in two cases to barren women who were thought to be too old to have children. The first of these was Isaac, the child of promise.

▶**Study Aim:** *To describe how God made, repeated, and kept His promise and how Abraham responded to the promise.*

STUDYING THE BIBLE

OUTLINE AND SUMMARY
    I.   **Promise Made (Gen. 15:1–16:16)**
          1. Divine revelation and human questions (15:1–3)
          2. God's promise and Abram's faith (15:4–6)
          3. Sarai, Hagar, and Ishmael (16:1–16)
    II. **Promise Repeated (Gen. 17:1–18:15)**
          1. Seeming delay in the promise (17:1–14)
          2. Seeming impossibility of the promise (17:15–27)
          3. Heavenly visitors (18:1–15)
    III. **Promise Kept (21:1–7)**

When God told Abram to fear not because God would reward him, Abram asked how (15:1–3). God promised a son to Abram and descendants as numerous as the stars, and Abram believed the Lord (15:4–21). Sarai initiated and later complained about Hagar becoming pregnant by Abram (16:1–16). When Abram was 99, the Lord repeated the promise and changed his name to Abraham (17:1–14). When Abraham laughed at the idea of him and Sarah having a son, the Lord gave the son's name and revealed the time of his birth (17:18–27). When Sarah overheard the Lord repeat the promise, she laughed (18:1–15). When Isaac was born as God had promised, Sarah laughed for joy (21:1–7).

I. Promise Made (Gen. 15:1–16:16)
1. Divine revelation and human questions (15:1–3)

1 After these things the word of the LORD came unto Abram in a vision, saying, Fear not, Abram: I am thy shield, and thy exceeding great reward.

2 And Abram said, LORD God, what wilt thou give me, seeing I go childless, and the steward of my house is this Eliezer of Damascus?

3 And Abram said, Behold, to me thou hast given no seed: and, lo, one born in my house is mine heir.

"These things" probably refer to the events of chapters 13–14. If so, this explains the Lord's promise of Abram's reward. Abram had given Lot the best of the land (Gen. 13). And after the Lord gave him victory over the kings who had captured Lot, Abram worshiped the Lord when he met Melchizedek; but he refused any part of the spoil from the king of Sodom (Gen. 14:17–24).

The formula "the word of the LORD came" is found throughout the Old Testament, especially to prophets when it came through a vision. God's word to "fear not" is also common in the Bible. Sometimes the people needed to be told not to fear God or His angel. In other cases, they were told not to fear dangers and uncertainties. The latter seems to have been the case with Abram. God promised to be his shield (Ps. 3:3). His words in verses 2–3 show he was anxious about the future and what it held.

Genesis 15:2–3 records the first words of Abram to the Lord. Significantly, the first words of this great man of faith were questions addressed to God. Bible people of faith were very candid in asking questions and expressing doubts to God. When these were addressed to God, He was patient with the questioner.

Abram remembered God's earlier promises (Gen. 12), but he had seen no evidence of fulfillment of the promises. The key to the whole issue was for Abraham to have a son; but Sarah was barren, and they both were growing older. At that time, Abram had named one of his faithful servants, Eliezer (see 24:2) as his heir. This could be legally done when a man had no actual son, although Abram and his descendants considered it a poor option.

2. God's promise and Abram's faith (15:4–6)

> **4 And behold, the word of the LORD came unto him, saying, This shall not be thine heir; but he that shall come forth out of thine own bowels shall be thine heir.**
>
> **5 And he brought him forth abroad, and said, Look now toward heaven, and tell the stars, if thou be able to number them: and he said unto him, So shall thy seed be.**
>
> **6 And he believed in the LORD; and he counted it to him for righteousness.**

God's reply in verse 4 is emphatic. Eliezer would not be Abram's heir. Abram's own son would be his heir. As a sign of this promise, God told Abram to look toward the clear night sky and count the stars. God promised that Abram's descendants would be as numerous as the stars.

Verse 6 is the key verse in the passage and one of the key verses in the Bible. Both Paul (Rom. 4:3; Gal. 3:6) and James (2:23) quote this verse as highlighting Abraham's faith. The word translated "believed" means to be firm or certain. It meant that Abram fixed himself firmly on the Lord and His promises. As quoted in the New Testament, it reads, "Abraham believed God" (Rom. 4:3). His was personal faith and trust in God, not just some beliefs about God.

How can we account for such faith on the part of a man who had just been asking God questions? For one thing, Abram had already exercised faith by coming to the promised land; so faith was not something new to him. In each case, Abram had only the promise of the unseen God about something as yet unfulfilled. In such circumstances, many people say, "Seeing is believing"; and refuse to believe in something they can't see or count. Abram, however, dared to believe God and His promise.

Paul makes much of the last part of the verse. He sees this verse as Old Testament support for the doctrine of justification by faith. Sinners cannot become righteous enough to become acceptable to God, but through Christ we can trust God's grace to pardon and keep us. God accepted Abram on the basis not of his good life but on the basis of his faith.

Yet even a person of such faith still asks questions. When God promised again that Abram would inherit Canaan, Abram wanted God to tell him how he could know that he would (15:7–8). God used an animal split in two as a covenant ceremony to seal His promise to Abram (15:9–21).

3. Sarai, Hagar, and Ishmael (16:1–16)

Sarai and Abram had waited ten years for the promise to be fulfilled. Then Sarai decided to take matters into her own hands. Following a custom of the day, she gave her maid to Abram as a kind of wife. Hagar was given to Abram with the understanding that her child would be counted as Sarai's (16:1–3; see Gen. 30:3, 9). Later when Hagar became pregnant, Sarai complained that she was arrogant and had Abram force Hagar to leave the camp (16:4–6). However, the Lord protected Hagar and enabled Ishmael to be born (16:10–16).

II. Promise Repeated (Gen. 17:1–18:15)

1. Seeming delay in the promise (17:1–14)

Notice the references to Abram's age in 12:4 (75), 16:16 (86), and 17:1 (99). Many years had passed, and Sarai was still barren when the Lord repeated to Abram the promise to multiply him exceedingly (17:2). Abram responded by falling to the ground (17:3). The Lord changed his name to Abraham and repeated the promise of an everlasting covenant (17:4–8). Then God instituted circumcision as a sign of the covenant (17:9–14).

2. Seeming impossibility of the promise (17:15–27)

17 Then Abraham fell upon his face, and laughed, and said in his heart, Shall a child be born unto him that is an hundred years old? and shall Sarah, that is ninety years old, bear?

18 And Abraham said unto God, O that Ishmael might live before thee!

19 And God said, Sarah thy wife shall bear thee a son indeed; and thou shalt call his name Isaac; and I will establish my covenant with him for an everlasting covenant, and with his seed after him.

20 And as for Ishmael, I have heard thee: Behold, I have blessed him, and will make him fruitful, and multiply him

exceedingly; twelve princes shall he beget, and I will make him a great nation.

21 But my covenant will I establish with Isaac, which Sarah shall bear unto thee at this set time in the next year.

God changed Sarai's name to Sarah, and promised that she would bear a son, through whom she would become mother of many nations (17:15–16). Hearing this, Abraham fell to the ground and laughed to himself at the promise of a man of 100 and a wife of 90 having a son. How can we explain Abraham's laughter?

Abraham's Ages at Crucial Times in His Life

75 When he left Haran for Canaan (12:4)
86 When Ishmael was born (16:16)
99 When God repeated the promise (17:1)
99 When Abraham was circumcised (17:24)
100 When Isaac was born (21:5)
175 When Abraham died (25:7)

Some Bible students think it was an exultant laugh of joy as was Sarah's laugh after Isaac was born (21:6). If so, verse 18 was a request that God not forget Ishmael. Other Bible students think that Abraham laughed at the sheer impossibility of what God was promising. The promise had sounded impossible 25 years earlier, when he was 75 and Sarah was 65; but now she was 90 and he was 100! If this is why he laughed, verse 18 represents a sincere request that God would accept Abraham's son Ishmael as the one through whom to achieve His purposes.

In either case, God dealt patiently with Abraham. We saw earlier how God dealt gently with Abram's sincere questions (15:2–3). If Abraham laughed in startled amazement tinged with some doubt, God was willing to accept that. Centuries later, Jesus responded to the sincere prayer of a man who prayed, "Lord, I believe; help thou mine unbelief" (Mark 9:24).

The Lord emphatically denied that Ishmael was to be the heir of the promise. He insisted that Sarah would bear a son. God promised not to forget Ishmael, who would have a nation of his own; however, God's covenant would be with the son of Abraham and Sarah. Additional information is given about the son. His name would be Isaac. He would have God's covenant established with him and his descendants. He would be born at the set time in the next year. Abraham showed his obedient faith by circumcising Ishmael and all the males in his household (17:22–27).

3. Heavenly visitors (18:1–15)

Three travelers showed up at Abraham's tent. The old man welcomed them and issued orders for a feast to be prepared (18:1–8). Since Genesis 18:1 says, "The LORD appeared unto him," at some point Abraham realized that one of the three was the Lord and the other two were angels (see Abraham's intercessory prayer in 18:16–33). Sarah was out of sight, but she heard the Lord repeat the promise that she would bear a son (18:9–10). Because of her age, Sarah laughed to herself (18:11–12). The

Lord asked why Sarah laughed (18:13). He said, "Is any thing too hard for the LORD?" (18:14). Then He promised that during the next spring, Sarah would have a son (18:14). Meanwhile, Sarah denied that she had laughed; but the Lord said that she did laugh (18:15).

III. Promise Kept (Gen. 21:1–7)

1 And the Lord visited Sarah as he had said, and the Lord did unto Sarah as he had spoken.

2 For Sarah conceived, and bare Abraham a son in his old age, at the set time of which God had spoken to him.

Verse 1 leaves no doubt that this was a miracle from God. The verse also emphasizes that God acted according to what He had promised. Verse 2 adds that He acted at the time He had promised. We may often think God is delaying His promises, but He doesn't operate on our time schedules. We may realize that the fulfillment of His promises are impossible by human standards, but is anything impossible for the Creator of all things?

Abraham named his son Isaac and circumcised him as God had commanded (21:3–4). Abraham was one hundred years old when Isaac was born (21:5). Once again, Sarah laughed; but this time there is no doubt that she laughed in exultant joy at what God had done (21:6–7).

SUMMARY OF BIBLE TRUTHS

1. When God is with us, we need not fear.
2. God is patient with honest questions addressed to Him.
3. Faith is trusting God and His promises.
4. God's promises sometimes seem delayed.
5. God's promises are often impossible by human standards.
6. God keeps His promises in His own way and time.

APPLYING THE BIBLE

1. A lesson in learning. A boy asked his father, "Dad, why is the sky blue?" His father replied, "I don't know, son." The boy asked, "Why is fire hot?" Again, the father said he didn't know. The boy posed a third question: "Why does the sun rise in the east?" And again, the father responded, "Son, I'm not sure about that." The boy said, "Sorry, dad, I don't mean to bother you with all these questions." To which the father said, "It's OK, son; how're you ever gonna learn if you don't ask questions?" God did not respond to Abraham that way! He told him, and reiterated several times, precisely what He intended to do through Abraham.

2. Once is enough. I was once participating in an ordaining council in which a young man was being questioned in preparation for his ordination. When asked what he believed about the virgin birth of Christ, he said, "Well, you know, only two gospel writers make explicit reference to it." To which an older man quietly asked, "Young man, how many times does God have to say a thing before you believe it?" Although God told Abraham several times what He intended to do through him, Abraham believed Him the very first time he heard it, even though, of course, he did not fully understand the implications of the promises of God.

3. Patience. A very important facet of following God, as Abraham and all other people of faith find out, is the matter of having patience. The walk of faith must learn to wait!

A young man came into my office the other day and told me he is having a very difficult time waiting for God to act. A young woman called me on the telephone yesterday with the same problem. I have, for years, given this counsel: We must give God four things when we are waiting for Him to act on one of His promises: (a) The thing itself, (b) Trust, (c) Time, and (d) Thanks. We may give Him more, but those represent irreducible minimums in the walk of faith.

4. Thoughts on faith.
▶ Faith needs wings, but it also needs landing gears.
▶ "The reason why birds can fly and we can't is simply that they have perfect faith, for to have faith is to have wings" (J. M. Barrie, "The Pocket Book of Quotations, New York: Pocket Books, 1942, p. 84).
▶ In modern liberalism "faith's wings are clipped by reason's scissors."
▶ "Without faith man becomes sterile, hopeless, and afraid to the very core of his being" (Erich Fromm).

5. Faith and reason. Robert Browning, in his poem "A Death In the Desert," has these famous lines:

> I say, the acknowledgement of God in Christ,
> Accepted by the reason, solves for thee
> All questions in the earth and out of it.

Well, what do you think? Of course, acknowledging God in Christ solves for us all questions, but "accepted by the reason" is precisely what faith is not. To be sure, our faith, like Abraham's, is built on solid and substantial facts, but the act of faith is, in the nature of the case, beyond reason. The "acknowledgement of God in Christ" cannot, in any biblical sense, be accepted by the reason apart from faith instructing it.

6. A great scientist speaks on faith. Blaise Pascal (1623–1662) speaks to that point:
▶ "The heart has its reasons of which reason knows nothing."[1]
▶ "It is the heart which perceives God and not the reason. That is what faith is: God perceived by the heart, not by the reason."[2]
▶ "Reason's last step is the recognition that there are an infinite number of things which are beyond it. It is merely feeble if it does not go so far as to realize that."[3]

All that from one of the keenest scientific minds that ever existed! That does not deny, as Pascal says somewhere else, that the mind must finally think through what the heart believes, but belief—he consistently maintained—begins in the heart.

7. Christ the solid rock.

> "When darkness seems to hide His face,
> I rest on His unchanging grace;
> In every high and stormy gale, my anchor holds
> within the veil."

8. Quick Quotes.

▶ "To believe means to recognize that we must wait until the veil shall be removed" (Anonymous).

▶ "Perhaps there is only one cardinal sin: impatience. Because of impatience we were driven out of Paradise; because of impatience we cannot return" (Franz Kafka).

▶ "Knowing this first, that there shall come in the last days scoffers, walking after their own lusts, and saying, Where is the promise of his coming? for since the fathers fell asleep, all things continue as they were from the beginning of the creation. For this they willingly (!) are ignorant of." "The Lord is not slack concerning his promise, as some men count slackness; but is longsuffering to us-ward, not willing that any should perish, but that all should come to repentance" (2 Pet. 3:3–5, 9). When God waits, there is always a reason!

TEACHING THE BIBLE

▶ *Main Idea:* God fulfills His promises on His schedule not ours.
▶ *Suggested Teaching Aim:* To lead adults to identify ways God has kept His promises to them.

A TEACHING OUTLINE

A Promise Fulfilled

1. *Promise Made (Gen. 15:1–16:16)*
2. *Promise Repeated (Gen. 17:1–18:15)*
3. *Promise Kept (Gen. 21:1–7)*

Introduce the Bible Study

Ask, How many great stages of divine work in the Bible began with the birth of a baby? (Jesus, Isaac, Moses, Samuel, John the Baptist.) Say, Today's lesson describes the way God fulfilled His promise to Abraham.

Search for Biblical Truth

IN ADVANCE, enlist two readers to read aloud alternately the seven summary statements in "Outline and Summary."

IN ADVANCE, copy the title and three points in "A Teaching Outline." Place the title and first point on the wall.

Be certain all members have a Bible. Ask the reader to read the first summary statement. Ask members to open their Bibles to Genesis 15:1–3 and find Abram's great concern. (He had no heir.) Ask: God instructed Abram to "fear not"; can you think of other times this message is given in the Bible around the birth of a child? (Birth of Jesus: Luke 1:13, 20; 2:10.) What did God mean by referring to Himself as "shield" and "great reward"? How is the "shield" related to God's command to "fear not"? Who had Abram designated as his heir? (Eliezer.)

IN ADVANCE, make a poster of 15:6 and place it on the wall. Ask the reader to read the second summary statement. Ask members to turn to 15:4–6 and find how God responded to Abram's response. (Counted it as righteousness.) Ask: What part do you think faith had in Isaac's birth? Did Abram and Sarai have a choice? In what other ways had Abram exercised faith?

DISCUSS: How do you respond to the statement, "We mustn't question God"? Can you think of great leaders in the Bible who did question God? Can you think of any who did not?

Ask the readers to read the third, fourth, and fifth summary statements. Place the second point of the outline on the wall. Ask members to turn to 17:17–21 and find Abraham's reaction to God's promise. (He laughed.)

Using the chart on page 45, show how Abraham's and Sarah's ages created a human problem.

Lecture briefly to explain the two possible interpretations of Abraham's laughter: (1) exultant laugh of joy; (2) laughed at the sheer impossibility of what God was promising.

Ask the readers to read the sixth and seventh summary statement. Place the third point of the outline on the wall. Ask members to turn to 21:1–7 and find how we can know this was a miraculous birth. (Members may suggest other correct statements, but the birth was at the "set time of which God had spoken.") Ask if anyone knows the meaning of the name *Isaac?* (Laughter.)

Read the six statements in "Summary of Bible Truths" and ask: Which one of these means the most to you? Why? Which statement is the most difficult for you to accept? Why?

Give the Truth a Personal Focus

Ask, How has God moved in your life when humanly speaking you could not find a solution to the problem you were facing? What promises has God made to you? Has He kept them all? Read statement 6 in "Summary of Bible Truths" to remind members that God does keep His promises, but in His own way and time.

---

1. Blaise Pascal, *Pensees* (London: Penguin Books, 1995), 127.
2. Ibid., 127.
3. Ibid., 56.

A Test of Faith

Background Passage: Genesis 22:1–19
Focal Passages: Genesis 22:1–2, 4–14

Abraham is mentioned as an example of faith by Paul, James, and the author of Hebrews. In the roll call of faith in Hebrews 11, Abraham is given more attention than any other Old Testament person. Three examples of his faith are magnified: his obedient faith in response to God's call (Heb. 11:8–10), his trust that God would give him and Sarah a child in their old age (Heb. 11:11–12), and his test of faith in being told to offer Isaac as a sacrifice (Heb. 11:17–19). These three correspond to the three lessons on Abraham, the third of which is the basis for this study.

▶**Study Aim:** *To explain why God's command to sacrifice Isaac was the ultimate test of Abraham's faith.*

STUDYING THE BIBLE

OUTLINE AND SUMMARY
I. **God Tested Abraham (Gen. 22:1–2)**
II. **Abraham Obeyed and Trusted (Gen. 22:3–10)**
   1. **Abraham obeyed God's word (22:3–4)**
   2. **Abraham trusted God completely (22:5–10)**
III. **God Provided (Gen. 22:11–19)**
   1. **God commended Abraham (22:11–12)**
   2. **God provided a substitute (22:13–14)**
   3. **God repeated the promise (22:15–19)**

God tested Abraham by telling him to offer Isaac as a burnt offering (22:1–2). Abraham obeyed God's word (22:3–4). He trusted God to provide (22:5–10). God's angel stopped Abraham and commended him for fearing God (22:11–12). Abraham offered a ram instead of Isaac (22:13–14). God repeated His covenant promises (22:15–19).

I. God Tested Abraham (Gen. 22:1–2)

1 And it came to pass after these things, that God did tempt Abraham, and said unto him, Abraham: and he said, Behold, here I am.

2 And he said, Take now thy son, thine only son Isaac, whom thou lovest, and get thee into the land of Moriah; and offer him there for a burnt offering upon one of the mountains which I will tell thee of.

The word translated "did tempt" can also mean "tested." Both the Hebrew word in the Old Testament and the Greek word in the New Testament can mean either "test" or "tempt." Only the context helps us decide which was meant. James 1:13 uses the Greek word to say that God never tempts anyone to do evil.

Abraham's test is stated in verse 2. What a thunderbolt from heaven this was! Nothing is said of Abraham's feelings when he heard this clear word from the Lord, but he understood immediately what this meant. Abraham knew that burnt offerings were offerings that were slain and then totally burned by fire. Abraham also knew that many pagan people practiced child sacrifice as a way of showing devotion to their god.

In fact, some people refuse to believe that God actually would have told Abraham to do so despicable a thing. It seems to contradict all the Bible tells us about a loving God. At other places, the Old Testament strongly condemned the practice (Lev. 18:21; 20:2–5; Deut. 12:30–31; 2 Kings 21:6). Thus, some people think that this was actually Abraham's idea, which he thought was God's will for him to show his devotion to the one true God. However, the Bible text clearly says that God told Abraham to do this. Isn't it unlikely that Abraham would ever have considered such a thing if God had not clearly told him to do it?

The wording of the command shows that God was sensitive to just how much He was asking. Notice the threefold repetition of what Isaac meant to Abraham. Isaac was his son, his only son, his son whom he loved deeply. In passing we may note that Ishmael was also Abraham's son, but he was not the son of promise through whom God had promised to bless all nations. However, this was more of a test than asking a father to sacrifice his beloved son. Because Isaac was the miracle child born in the old age of Abraham and Sarah and because he was Abraham's link with the future, Abraham was being asked to cut off his own future. When God called Abram to leave and go to Canaan, God asked him to give up his past. Now God was asking him to give up his future.

Yet it was not just Abraham's future and Isaac's; it was the future of all that God had promised to do for all nations through the descendants of the child of promise. Thus, the test seemed to make impossible all the purposes of God. If Isaac were slain, what about the promise of divine blessing to all nations?

II. Abraham Obeyed and Trusted God (Gen. 22:3–10)

1. Abraham obeyed God's word (22:3–4)

4 Then on the third day Abraham lifted up his eyes, and saw the place afar off.

At no point in Genesis 22:1–14 are we told Abraham's thoughts. We are told what he did. In other words, without a question or a complaint, Abraham immediately obeyed God's word. Other biblical personalities often asked questions or raised objections at such times, and Abraham asked questions at some points prior to this; however, as far as we know, he simply obeyed.

The journey took three days; therefore, he had three long days to consider what he was doing and turn back. The fact that he started right away and kept going for three days is sure proof of total obedience to God.

2. Abraham trusted God completely (22:5–10)

5 And Abraham said unto his young men, Abide ye here with the ass; and I and the lad will go yonder and worship, and come again to you.

When they arrived at a certain point, Abraham left his two servants with the pack animal. He told them that he and Isaac were going up the mountain to worship. Notice the words "and come again to you." This is the first of the mysteries of what Abraham expected to happen. He was fully prepared to kill Isaac and planned to do so. However, he told the two servants that Isaac would come back down the mountain with him. Hebrews 11:17–19 says that Abraham believed that God could raise Isaac from the dead.

6 And Abraham took the wood of the burnt offering, and laid it upon Isaac his son; and he took the fire in his hand, and a knife, and they went both of them together.

7 And Isaac spake unto Abraham his father, and said, My father: and he said, Here am I, my son. And he said, Behold the fire and the wood: but where is the lamb for a burnt offering?

8 And Abraham said, My son, God will provide himself a lamb for a burnt offering: so they went both of them together.

9 And they came to the place which God had told him of; and Abraham built an altar there, and laid the wood in order, and bound Isaac his son, and laid him on the altar upon the wood.

10 And Abraham stretched forth his hand, and took the knife to slay his son.

What was Isaac's part in all this? We can only speculate how old he was. The translation "lad" seems to make him only a boy; yet the same Hebrew word is translated "young men" for the two servants. All we can say for sure is that he was either a boy or a young man. He was old enough to carry the wood.

At some point, Isaac began to wonder about what his father planned to do. Finally, he asked the obvious question about the absence of a sacrificial animal. Abraham's answer expressed Abraham's faith that the Lord would somehow provide. We read of no other questions from Isaac. He probably realized he was the intended sacrifice even before Abraham bound him and placed him on the wood of the altar.

Although the Bible does not say anything about Isaac's trust, the text shows the mutual love and respect of father and son. This is seen in the words "my father" and "my son" that they used when they spoke. It is seen in the clause "they went both of them together." Above all, it is seen in Isaac's voluntary submission to his father's plans for him. He obviously trusted his father and likely shared his father's faith in God.

The word translated "provide" is usually translated "see" in the Bible. It is translated "seen" in verse 14. Some scholars have suggested that the word is used in the sense of "see ahead" or "see beforehand." Our word "provide" comes from a prefix for "before" and a word meaning "see" (we get our word "video" from it"). The same scholars point out that the word *providence* is from the same two words. Thus, Abraham was expressing faith in the providence of God. This is the biblical doctrine that God is at work to accomplish His good purpose. This kind of trust in the wisdom and goodness of God is essential for faith that passes the kind of test that Abraham faced. The outward circumstances seemed to deny that God was good and that His purposes would be fulfilled; yet Abraham dared to trust God to do whatever was necessary to vindicate His goodness and to achieve His purposes.

III. God Provided (Gen. 22:11–19)

1. God commended Abraham (22:11–12)

11 And the angel of the LORD called unto him out of heaven, and said, Abraham, Abraham: and he said, Here am I.

12 And he said, Lay not thine hand upon the lad, neither do thou any thing unto him: for now I know that thou fearest God, seeing thou hast not withheld thy son, thine only son from me.

The angel of the Lord in the Old Testament is so closely associated with God that He speaks at times as God. Some people think He was the second person of the Trinity. At any rate, God stopped Abraham just in time, commanded him not to harm Isaac, and commended him. Abraham obviously passed the test. The Bible uses the word *fear* in relationship to God to describe total commitment and obedience to the Lord.

2. God provided a substitute (22:13–14)

13 And Abraham lifted up his eyes, and looked, and behold behind him a ram caught in a thicket by his horns: and Abraham went and took the ram, and offered him up for a burnt offering in the stead of his son.

14 And Abraham called the name of that place Jehovah-jireh: as it is said to this day, In the mount of the LORD it shall be seen.

At just the right time, the Lord did provide. Abraham saw the ram caught in the thicket and offered it as the burnt offering "in the stead of his son." The ram became a substitute for Isaac. The ram died so that Abraham's only beloved son would not have to die. Christians cannot fail to see in this a foreshadowing of God giving His only Son to die as a substitute for sinners, so that we will not have to die the death our sins deserve. Those who see God's command to Abraham as a lack of love on God's part need to remember that God the Father *did* what He *did not* allow Abraham to carry out. He gave His only Son as a sacrifice.

Although the word *seen* is used in our translation, other translators use "provided," since it is the same word translated "provide" in verse 8. Isaac's question, "Where is the lamb?" was immediately answered by Abraham, "God will provide himself a lamb." Short-range, the substitute God provided was a ram. Long-range, the answer to Isaac's question is "Behold, the Lamb of God, which taketh away the sin of the world" (John 1:29).

What then was achieved by the traumatic test of Abraham's faith? Abraham and his son Isaac were the key links in God's chain of redemption. Their faith had to be strong enough to fulfill that strategic role. This test purified and strengthened the already remarkable faith of Abraham. God's plan could be built securely on his place as father of the faithful.

3. God repeated the promise (22:15–19)

The Lord renewed the covenant promise on the basis of Abraham's willingness to offer Isaac (22:15–16). God promised to bless Abraham with many descendants and to bless all nations through His seed (22:17–18). Abraham, Isaac, and the young men then returned to their camp (22:19).

SUMMARY OF BIBLE TRUTHS

1. God tests people of faith—the stronger the faith, the greater the test.
2. Some of God's tests seem to be contrary to His goodness and to our own best interests.
3. When God's word is clear, people of faith obey.
4. Faith involves trusting God completely.
5. God will do what is necessary to achieve His good purpose.
6. God gave His only Son as a substitute sacrifice for our sins.

APPLYING THE BIBLE

1. God's insurance. Lloyd's of London has written some interesting insurance policies, including these:

▶ A $100,000 "love insurance" policy that pledged payment if a photographer's model married (she did, but after the policy expired);

▶ A "happiness policy" that insured against "worry lines" developing on a model's face;

▶ Protection (the premium was $74.00) against death caused by a falling "sputnik," and various others such as policies insuring against the chances of having twins, of one's golf opponent making a hole in one, and of having a church social rained out.[1]

When God makes a promise to one of His servants, such as He did to Abraham, no insurance is needed to guarantee it because there is not one chance in a million of God's promise not coming true. The Bible, from one cover to the other, is a commentary on the truth of Titus 1:2, "God ... cannot lie." The writer of Hebrews refers to that fact when he says, of God's promises to Abraham: "For when God made promise to Abraham, because he could swear by no greater, he sware by himself" (Heb. 6:13).

2. God built a bridge. Somebody told a great story about a little girl describing her first train ride. She said, "We came to a lake and I was 'most scared to death. We ran right into it, but it was all right. Somebody had gone ahead and built a bridge over it!" That is a perfect description, as Abraham learned, of providence. "Providence" means, literally, "to see before." Which is precisely what God does. About everything!

3. Acting in faith. Abraham literally had to risk all in faith to please and obey God. For discussion: How do we attempt to take the "sting" out of faith, reducing it to something innocuous and safe, a "be kind to granny and the cat" sort of thing? (How do we "hedge" our bet?) Abraham's faith is not that which marks a person entering into the faith, but that which marks a mature and longtime believer. Must mature Christians continue to exercise faith? In what kinds of circumstances? Why? Does acting on faith build one's faith? How and why? How is God honored in our faith? What difference could it make to Him whether we act in faith or not? Where is it that God is now asking you to act in faith?

4. God gave His Son as a substitute for us. That, of course, is at the heart of the biblical doctrine of salvation. In the year 1585 an event happened that illustrates the truth of substitution. "There was another of those, that in Portugal are called New Christians. He being allotted to be thrown overboard in the sea, had a younger brother in the same boat, that suddenly rose up and desired the Captain that he would pardon and make free his brother, and let him supply his place, saying, 'My brother is older, and of better knowledge in the world than I, and therefore more fit to live in the world, and to help my sisters and friends in their need: so that I had rather die for him, than to live without him.' At which request, they let the elder brother loose, and threw the younger at his own request into the sea." The story does not end as does that of the Savior, though. The young man swam for about six hours alongside the boat and "in the end, they were constrained to take him in again." When Jesus was told to come down from the cross, even though He could have, He chose not to. And thus, was able to accomplish our salvation.[2]

5. An easy cross. An exclusive jewelry store in New York once displayed a fabulous collection of exquisite crosses for sale. Underneath the display of crosses was this statement: "These Crosses on Easy Terms."

6. A substitute. The theologian Charles Hodge said, "Vicarious suffering is suffering endured by one person in the stead of another, i.e., in his place. It necessarily supposes the exemption of the party in whose place the suffering is endured. A *vicar* is a substitute, one who takes the place of another, and acts in his stead."[3]

TEACHING THE BIBLE

▶ *Main Idea:* God tests our faith so we will know how much we trust Him.

▶ *Suggested Teaching Aim:* To lead adults to analyze how much they trust God.

A TEACHING OUTLINE

A Test of Faith

1. *God Tested Abraham (Gen. 22:1–2)*
2. *Abraham Obeyed and Trusted (Gen. 22:3–10)*
3. *God Provided (Gen. 22:11–19)*

Introduce the Bible Study

Use illustration #2 from "Applying the Bible" to introduce the lesson. Read the Main Idea and point out that Abraham had three great demonstrations of his faith: (1) obeyed God's call, (2) believed God would provide a son, and (3) willing to sacrifice Isaac. Point out that today's lesson covers this last demonstration.

Search for Biblical Truth

Ask a volunteer to read aloud Genesis 22:1–2. Ask members to share what word their different translations have for "tempt" (KJV, 22:1). (Some translations: "prove"—ASV; "put to the test"—Torah; "tried"—Septuagint.) Ask: Which word do you think works best here? Why?

Ask, Why do you think God felt this experience was necessary? Was this for God's benefit or for Abraham's? On a chalkboard or a large sheet of paper write: *What made sacrificing Isaac so hard?* Ask members to share their answers. Possible answers: Isaac was his only son of promise; they had waited so long for Isaac; Isaac was the key to the future for Abraham and Sarah; Abraham had given up his past when he moved to Canaan; sacrificing Isaac meant giving up his future too.)

Ask a volunteer to read 22:4. On a map of the Old Testament, locate Hebron. Suggest that Abraham lived somewhere in this general area. Suggest that Moriah, the place of sacrifice, may have been where Jerusalem is located now. Ask: How long did it take Abraham to reach Moriah? (Three days.) Did a journey of three days make it difficult or easier for Abraham? Why?

Ask members to read silently 22:5 several times. Ask, What in this verse describes Abraham's hope? ("We will come again.") Ask someone to read Hebrews 11:17–19. Ask, Based on this passage, how did Abraham expect God to respond? (To raise Isaac from the dead.)

Ask members to read silently 22:6–10. Distribute paper and pencils to each person. Ask half the class to write down what they think Abraham was thinking and the other half to write down what they think Isaac was thinking during this whole process.

Ask a volunteer to read aloud 22:11–12. Point out that the "angel" of the Lord is so closely associated with God that He speaks at times as God. Point out in verse 11, the voice is identified as the voice of the "angel"; in verse 12, the "me" would refer to God Himself.

Ask members to read silently 22:13–14. Ask: What was achieved by the traumatic test of Abraham's faith? Why do you think God tested them so fiercely?

IN ADVANCE, write out the six "Summary of Bible Truths" on small slips of paper. Organize members into six groups and give each group one of the truths. Ask members to: (1) discuss if they believe this statement and why; (2) identify an area in their lives to which this statement would give them guidance.

Give the Truth a Personal Focus

Ask members to continue in their groups and answer these questions: How much do you trust God? What evidence can you cite that you trust God? Can you share an example when it seemed God's testing was contrary to His goodness and to your own best interests?

Close in prayer that all would see God as a caring Father whom they can trust completely.

---

1. *The People's Almanac,* ed. by Wallechinsky and Wallace (Garden City, N.Y.: Doubleday and Company, 1975), 352–353.

2. John Careyt, *Eyewitness to History* (New York: Avon Books, 1978), 134.

3. Quoted in H. C. Thiessen, *Lectures in Systematic Theology* (Grand Rapids: Wm. B. Eerdmans Publishing Company, 1956), 321.

Deceit and Blessing

Background Passages: Genesis 25:19–34; 27:1–40
Focal Passages: Genesis 25:29–34; 27:30–37

Genesis 25:19 introduces the section of Genesis on the "generations of Isaac," which extends to 37:1; however, Jacob is actually the main personality in most of these chapters. This lesson focuses on two early incidents in Jacob's life: buying the birthright from Esau and deceiving Isaac into giving Jacob the blessing.

▶**Study Aim:** *To describe how Jacob got the birthright and the blessing.*

STUDYING THE BIBLE

OUTLINE AND SUMMARY

I. **Rivalry Between Esau and Jacob (Gen. 25:19–28)**
   1. **Rivalry before birth (25:19–26)**
   2. **Rivalry in life (25:27–28)**

II. **The Birthright (Gen. 25:29–34)**
   1. **Esau's hunger, Jacob's deal (25:29–31)**
   2. **Jacob's coolness, Esau's impulsiveness (25:32–34)**

III. **The Blessing (Gen. 27:1–40)**
   1. **Isaac's plan and Rebekah's plot (27:1–17)**
   2. **Jacob's deception of Isaac (27:18–29)**
   3. **Isaac's anguish (27:30–33)**
   4. **Esau's accusations and plea (27:34–40)**

Before Esau and Jacob were born, God predicted that Jacob would be dominant (25:19–26). Parental favoritism was a factor in the rivalry of the twins (25:27–28). When Esau was hungry, Jacob offered him food in exchange for Esau's birthright (25:29–31). The impulsive Esau agreed to the deal (25:32–34). Isaac planned to give his blessing to Esau, but Rebekah plotted how to get the blessing for Jacob (27:1–17). Jacob pretended to be Esau and deceived his blind father (27:18–29). When Isaac discovered the deception, he was in deep anguish because he knew that the blessing could not be canceled (27:30–33). Esau said that Jacob had supplanted him two times, and he pleaded for Isaac to give him a blessing (27:34–40).

I. Rivalry of Esau and Jacob (Gen. 25:19–28)

1. Rivalry before birth (25:19–26)

Because Rebekah was barren, Isaac prayed for her to conceive; and the Lord answered the prayer (25:19–21). Feeling the children struggling within her, Rebekah asked the Lord why (25:22). The Lord told her that two nations struggled within her, and He predicted that the older would serve the younger (25:23). When they were born, Esau the older twin was red and covered with hair; Jacob the younger grasped Esau's heel (25:24–26).

2. Rivalry in life (25:27–28)

Esau and Jacob came into the world different in appearance, temperament, and destiny. Esau became a hunter, an outdoorsman. Jacob lived a quieter life, often staying inside the tents (25:27). The built-in differences were heightened by parental favoritism. Isaac loved Esau, and Rebekah loved Jacob (25:28).

II. The Birthright (Gen. 25:29–34)

1. Esau's hunger, Jacob's deal (25:29–31)

29 And Jacob sod pottage: and Esau came in from the field, and he was faint.

30 And Esau said to Jacob, Feed me, I pray thee, with that same red pottage; for I am faint: therefore was his name called Edom.

31 And Jacob said, Sell me this day thy birthright.

The incident began naturally enough. Jacob was in the tent cooking a stew made of lentils. Esau came in from the field. He was famished with hunger. He asked Jacob to feed him some of the red stew he was cooking. (The name "Edom" was the nation formed by Esau's descendants.) No doubt this had happened many times in the past. Jacob was the cook, and he no doubt often fed the hungry Esau. However, on this occasion, Jacob refused to give the stew to Esau. Instead, he offered to sell it to him.

Later the Law spelled out the birthright. Deuteronomy 21:15–17 commanded that the firstborn receive a position of strength and a double portion of the estate. During the time of the patriarchs, the firstborn in the family of Abraham often did not receive the birthright. Isaac was born after Ishmael, but Isaac received the birthright. God had already told Rebekah that this would be true of her two sons. In His sovereign way, God had chosen Jacob instead of Esau. Also in the family of Abraham, the birthright included not only headship of the family and the larger portion of the estate but also the promise to continue the line of promise.

We do not know whether Rebekah had told Jacob of the strange prophecy made before his birth. And even if she had, we do not know to what degree Jacob's actions were motivated by a desire for the spiritual aspects of the promise. Hebrews 11:21–22 says that Jacob was a man of faith, but the examples cited are from later in his life—when his faith was much more obvious than in the early part.

2. Jacob's coolness, Esau's impulsiveness (25:32–34)

32 And Esau said, Behold, I am at the point to die: and what profit shall this birthright do to me?

33 And Jacob said, Swear to me this day; and he sware unto him: and he sold his birthright unto Jacob.

34 Then Jacob gave Esau bread and pottage of lentils; and he did eat and drink, and rose up, and went his way: thus Esau despised his birthright.

In this situation, each of the two brothers acted as you would expect in light of what we know of the character of each. Esau, a man of physical appetites, said that he was starving to death right then. No doubt this was an overstatement. Jacob quickly seized on this expected response and promised to feed Esau on condition that Esau swear that he was trading his birthright for the pottage. In those days, an oath was completely binding (Josh. 9:19). Esau did not hesitate to make the deal.

Then Jacob gave him the stew, some bread, and something to drink. Esau gulped it down, "and rose up, and went his way." The only judgment rendered on the actions of either of the brothers is that by doing this, "Esau despised his birthright." Nothing is said about Jacob's shrewd dealing, but Esau was faulted for showing such little regard for his birthright.

Esau was an impulsive man who sought immediate satisfaction of whatever he wanted. Some future birthright seemed unimportant to such a man who had an opportunity to get something he wanted right then. Hebrews 12:15–17 says that he was a profane man. Today we might call him a secular man who lives only for the moment and for what he can see and count. Spiritual things are unimportant to him, especially if they apply only to the distant future.

Isaac—The Peaceful Patriarch

Isaac is far less prominent in the Bible than Abraham and Jacob. In most passages, Isaac is overshadowed either by his illustrious father or his active son.

III. The Blessing (Gen. 27:1–40)
1. Isaac's plan and Rebekah's plot (27:1–17)
The blessing in Isaac's family was the key part of the birthright. Isaac was determined to give the blessing to his firstborn. Thus, he sent Esau out to prepare a feast appropriate for giving the blessing (27:1–5).

Rebekah overheard this plan and involved Jacob in a bizarre plan of deception designed to thwart Isaac's plan and to secure the blessing for her favorite, Jacob (27:6–10). Jacob's only fear seems to have been that Isaac would become aware of the deception and curse rather than bless Jacob (27:11–12). Rebekah said that if that happened, let the curse fall on her (27:13). Then the two of them began to prepare to deceive Isaac (27:14–17).

2. Jacob's deception of Isaac (27:18–29)
The deception depended on Isaac's blindness and on Jacob having the right food and the right feel and smell to convince Isaac that he was Esau. Isaac was suspicious when his son returned so soon. With something approaching blasphemy, Jacob said that the Lord had led him quickly to the game (27:18–20). Isaac also was suspicious that the voice sounded more like Jacob than Esau; yet when he felt Jacob's arms, Isaac was fooled by the skins that had been tied on Jacob's arms. Then just to be sure, Isaac asked, "Art thou my very son Esau?" And Jacob again lied, "I am" (27:21–24). Then Isaac proceeded with the meal and pronounced on Jacob the blessing he intended for Esau (27:25–29).

3. Isaac's anguish (27:30–33)
30 And it came to pass, as soon as Isaac had made an end of blessing Jacob, and Jacob was yet scarce gone out from the

presence of Isaac his father, that Esau his brother came in from his hunting.

31 And he also had made savoury meat, and brought it unto his father, and said unto his father, Let my father arise, and eat of his son's venison, that thy soul may bless me.

32 And Isaac his father said unto him, Who art thou? And he said, I am thy son, thy firstborn Esau.

33 And Isaac trembled very exceedingly, and said, Who? where is he that hath taken venison, and brought it me, and I have eaten of all before thou camest, and have blessed him? yea, and he shall be blessed.

Just as Jacob left, Esau arrived. He was no doubt happy at the prospect of receiving the blessing. As yet, he was totally unsuspecting. Isaac also was unsuspecting until he heard Esau's voice. Then he knew that something was wrong. When Isaac began to quiz him, Esau also began to realize that something had gone wrong.

The intensity of Isaac's feelings is apparent from the description that he "trembled very exceedingly." In a moment, he realized that he had been tricked into giving the blessing to Jacob. And what made matters hopeless, the blessing, once spoken, could not be recalled or reversed. That is what Isaac meant when he said of Jacob the deceiver, "Yea, and he shall be blessed."

In our day, we may wonder why Isaac did not simply cancel the blessing since it was secured by lies and deception. The answer is that according to Hebrew reverence for words, this could not be done. Words were considered extensions of one's personality and power. Once spoken, words could not be recalled. Rebekah and Jacob knew that their deception would surely be discovered, but they also knew that the blessing now belonged forever to Jacob.

4. Esau's accusations and plea (27:34–40)

34 And when Esau heard the words of his father, he cried with a great and exceeding bitter cry, and said unto his father, Bless me, even me also, O my father.

35 And he said, Thy brother came with subtilty, and hath taken away thy blessing.

36 And he said, Is not he rightly named Jacob? for he hath supplanted me these two times: he took away my birthright; and, behold, now he hath taken away my blessing. And he said, Hast thou not reserved a blessing for me?

37 And Isaac answered and said unto Esau, Behold, I have made him thy lord, and all his brethren have I given to him for servants; and with corn and wine have I sustained him: and what shall I do now unto thee, my son?

The emotional Esau quickly responded. His response was twofold: he vented his wrath at the deception of Jacob, and he pleaded with Isaac to give him some blessing. Esau said that Jacob was rightly named Jacob. Originally, the name Jacob meant "God provides," but from birth this

Jacob was known as the supplanter—one who takes what belongs to another. Esau mentioned two examples: taking away the birthright and taking away the blessing. The former of these was a cunning deal, and Esau should have accepted his share of the blame for that. However, the blessing was more of a real example of deception.

Isaac finally gave Esau a blessing, but it was considerably less than what Jacob had received. Esau could take solace only in that someday his descendants would break free from Jacob's domination (27:38–40). Nowhere in the text is any of the four participants in this episode condemned, but later events show that each reaped a bitter harvest for his or her part in it. Yet through it (or perhaps in some ways in spite of it) God fulfilled his prophecy of making Jacob the heir of the promise to Abraham and to Isaac.

Isaac the Patriach

I.	During Abraham's Lifetime (Gen. 21:1–25:11)
1.	Born as the child of promise (21:1–7)
2.	Almost offered as a sacrifice by Abraham (22:1–19)
3.	Received a wife selected by Abraham (24:1–67)
4.	Buried Abraham (25:2–11)

II.	During Jacob's Lifetime (Gen. 25:19–37:1)
1.	Prayed for Rebekah to have a child (25:19–21)
2.	Showed partiality for Esau (25:28)
3.	In the only Bible chapter devoted to Isaac without reference to Abraham or Jacob, Isaac showed himself to be a man of peace. God blessed him with the respect of others and renewed the promise with him (26:1–33).
4.	Deceived by Rebekah and Jacob into giving Jacob the blessing Isaac intended for Esau (27:1–17)
5.	Gave Esau an inferior blessing (27:18–40)
6.	Blessed Jacob as he left for Haran (27:41–28:5)
7.	Displeased by Esau's marriage to pagans (28:6–9)
8.	Died and was buried by Jacob and Esau (35:27–29)

SUMMARY OF BIBLE TRUTHS

1. God acts with sovereign freedom in His choices.
2. Rivalry among brothers is common and can have serious consequences.
3. Acting impulsively and living for present gratification can have long-range bad results.
4. God works to accomplish his good purposes, sometimes even using actions and people that do wrong things.
5. Deception and betrayal destroy the basis for trust and loving relationships.
6. Words have more power than most people think.

APPLYING THE BIBLE

1. Broken promises. I heard about a seven-year-old boy who asked his second-grade teacher one day, "Teacher, suppose a man promised a girl a castle, a boat, a car, and marriage. Can she sue him for breaking his promise?" The teacher shook her head and said, "No, breach-of-promise cases are now outlawed in this state." His friend, aged eight, who sat next to the questioner, leaned over and said in his ear, "There you are, pal, I told you that you had nothing to worry about."[1] Both Jacob and Esau were to learn that words have much more effect than that!

2. Acting impulsively. Esau acted on the basis of fleshly instincts, and he paid for it for the rest of his life. That tendency to act impulsively is very pronounced in humans. It first appeared in Eden, where both Adam and Eve acted impulsively, at a tremendous cost to them and their progeny; and it is manifested many millions of times daily—to the sadness of a huge segment of the human population.

▶ "For fools rush in where angels fear to tread" (Alexander Pope).[2]

▶ "Their kitchen is their shrine, the cook their priest, the table their altar, and their belly their god."[3]

▶ "Whose end is destruction, whose God is their belly (appetite), and whose glory is in their shame, who mind earthly things" (Phil. 3:19).

▶ "If sensuality were happiness, beasts were happier than men; but human felicity is lodged in the soul, not in the flesh" (Seneca).

▶ "As Christians, we do not have to renounce everything that gives pleasure to the senses. But we do have to moderate our use of sense pleasures. Original sin has left us easy marks for the allurements of sense."[4]

▶ "I don't want the cheese; I just want out of the trap" (Portugese proverb).

3. The price of deception. Any deceptive act has within itself the seeds of tragedy. The Associated Press carried a story about a deception that shook the country. The U. S. Navy's top admiral, Jeremy Boorda, the chief of naval operations "grabbed a .38 caliber handgun that belonged to his son-in-law, walked outside, rested the gun barrel against his chest and pulled the trigger." He did so because he had falsified certain military reports enabling him to wear combat medals which he was not qualified to wear. His deception cost him his reputation and, in the end, his very life.[5] Sir Walter Scott said, for us all:

"Oh, what a tangled web we weave

When first we practice to deceive! ("Marmion," Canto VI, stanza 17).

4. For discussion:

▶ Do you think American culture is sensate—that is, that giving in to the impulses of the flesh marks us as a people?

▶ If so, what are the most obvious evidences?

▶ In your view, are Americans essentially any different in that regard from other peoples?

▶ Why does the old adage, "Before you speak, count to ten" make sense? How does that adage apply to certain laws that restrict the purchase of guns, or obtaining a divorce, etc., until a waiting period has been observed?

> The Bible says, "A brother offended is harder to be won than a strong city: and their contentions are like the bars of a castle" (Prov. 18:19). What specific steps could Esau and Jacob have taken to have voided their conflict? Which man should have acted first?

5. God's sovereign purpose. Our author reminds us that God sometimes uses wrong acts and the people who do them to accomplish His sovereign purpose. In fact, He has never used a perfect person yet to do something for Him. I love the story about a young woman who lived in a dirty run-down apartment and who was very hungry. She was a believer and prayed to God for help. The owner of the apartment was a cheat who hated God and his renters, too, but the young woman bore faithful witness to him. He heard her praying for food and thought he'd show her something once and for all about her God whom she trusted to provide. She came home one day and found, to her great surpise and joy, that God had answered her prayer. On her steps was a whole carload of groceries. She began praising God and went and told the landlord about her answered prayer. The man toyed with her a while and then announced the truth: He himself, and not her God, had bought the groceries. She laughed and said, "Oh, yes, God DID provide. He just used the devil to deliver them."[6]

Jacob wasn't quite as bad as that, but God still used him, in spite of his deceptive activity (and character!), in the process of blessing His people. The point for all of us: We must not wait until we—or others—are perfect before we submit ourselves to the sovereign God for His use in blessing others.

TEACHING THE BIBLE

> *Main Idea:* God can use our failures to accomplish His purpose.
> *Suggested Teaching Aim:* To lead adults to identify ways God has used even our failures to accomplish His purpose.

A TEACHING OUTLINE

Deceit and Blessing: Genesis 25:29–34; 27:30–37

1. *Rivalry between Esau and Jacob (25:19–28)*
2. *The Birthright (25:29–34)*
3. *The Blessing (27:1–40)*

Introduce the Bible Study

Share the illustration in #5 from "Applying the Bible," to introduce the lesson. Say, God can use anything or anyone—including our failures—to accomplish His purpose. Today's lesson will demonstrate how God used Jacob in spite of his deceit and treachery.

Search for Biblical Truth

IN ADVANCE, copy "A Teaching Outline" on four strips of paper. Place the title and the first point on the wall. Briefly summarize the material in Genesis 25:19–28 to establish the lesson's context and to describe Esau and Jacob.

IN ADVANCE, enlist two members to help you teach the lesson. Place three chairs at the front of the room for you and the participants. Give the participants one of the following assignments and have them to be prepared to answer the questions when you ask them. Place the outline points on the wall before each participant responds. After each presentation, let members ask questions of the participants. Copy the six statements in "Summary of Bible Truths" and give even-numbered statements to Participant 2 and the odd-numbered statements to Participant 1. (Instead of using the two participants to help you, you can use these questions as points in a lecture or to guide a group discussion.)

Participant 1: The Birthright (Gen. 25:29–34)

Study these verses and be prepared to answer the following questions. Keep in mind that the Main Idea of the lesson is "God can use our failures to accomplish His purpose." Be prepared to answer questions from the class after your presentation. Be sure you cover these specific points:

1. How did Jacob and Esau differ?
2. What was the birthright?
3. Who received the birthright in ancient Hebrew society?
4. What did the birthright in Abraham's family line indicate?
5. How did Esau despise his birthright?

Participant 2: The Blessing (Gen. 27:1–40)

Study these verses and be prepared to answer the following questions. Keep in mind that the Main Idea of the lesson is "God can use our deception to accomplish His purpose." Be prepared to answer questions from the class after your presentation. Be sure you cover these specific points:

1. Why did Isaac ask Esau to prepare him a meal?
2. Whose idea was the deception?
3. How did Rebekah calm Jacob's anxieties about the curse?
4. How did Jacob misuse God to further his trickery?
5. What was Jacob's blessing?
6. What was Esau's blessing?

Ask the two participants to read the six statements in "Summary of Bible Truths" to summarize the lesson.

Give the Truth a Personal Focus

Ask, Since God had chosen Jacob before his birth to be the one through whom Abraham's line would descend, was Jacob wrong in doing what he did to get the birthright and the blessing? Why? Ask members to share ways in which God has used their failures/misfortunes to accomplish His will.

---

1. James C. Humes, *Podium Humor* (New York: Harper Perennial, 1975), 70.

2. Quoted in *Familiar Quotations,* by John Bartlett, (Thirteenth edition, Little, Brown and Company, Boston and Toronto, 1955), 312.

3. Charles D. Buck in *Instant Quotation Dictionary,* edited by Donald Bolander (Mundelein, Ill.: Career Institute), 126.

4. John C. Ford in *The World Treasury of Religious Quotations,* ed. Ralph Woods (New York: Garland Books, 1966), 918.

5. *St. Petersberg Times,* 5/17/96, p. 1A.

6. Bill Glass, *How To Win When the Roof Caves In* (Old Tappan, New Jersey Fleming H. Revell, 1988), pp. 72–73. Quoted in Associated Press, St. Petersburg Times, 17 May 1966, 1–A.

Jacob's Flight and Vision

Background Passage: Genesis 27:41–28:22
Focal Passages: Genesis 27:41; 28:10–16,18–22

Up to this point in Jacob's life, the Bible has recorded no evidence of personal faith in God by Jacob—unless we assume that his desire for the birthright and blessing were spiritually motivated. Jacob's only recorded words about God are in Genesis 27:20, when he lied about God to cover up his deception of Isaac. Jacob referred to the Lord as "thy God," not "my God." When Jacob fled from Esau's anger, Jacob did not know that he was about to have his own encounter with God.

▶**Study Aim:** *To describe God's revelation to Jacob at Bethel and to analyze Jacob's responses.*

STUDYING THE BIBLE

OUTLINE AND SUMMARY
  I.   **Jacob's Flight (Gen. 27:41–28:9)**
       1. **Esau's anger (27:41)**
       2. **Rebekah's actions (27:42–46)**
       3. **Isaac's instructions and blessing (28:1–5)**
       4. **Esau's marriages (28:6–9)**
  II. **Jacob's Encounter with God (Gen. 28:10–22)**
       1. **Jacob's crisis (28:10–11)**
       2. **God's revelation (28:12–15)**
       3. **Jacob's initial responses (28:16–19)**
       4. **Jacob's vow (28:20–22)**

Esau planned to kill Jacob (27:41). Rebekah made plans to have Jacob sent to her family (27:42–46). Isaac blessed Jacob as he sent him to find a wife among his mother's family (28:1–5). Esau's marriages displeased Isaac (28:6–9). Jacob used a stone for a pillar when night came (28:10–11). God revealed Himself to Jacob in a dream and made him the heir of the promises to Abraham and Isaac (28:12–15). The surprised Jacob set up a pillar and named the place "house of God" (28:16–19). He made a vow that expressed his acceptance of God's promises (28:20–22).

I. Jacob's Flight (Gen. 27:41–28:9)

1. Esau's anger (27:41)

> **41 And Esau hated Jacob because of the blessing wherewith his father blessed him: and Esau said in his heart, The days of mourning for my father are at hand; then will I slay my brother Jacob.**

Verse 41 continues the story of deception in Genesis 27:1–40. This verse describes Esau's feelings and decision after he had been robbed of the blessing Isaac had promised to give him. Out of respect for his father, Esau planned to postpone his actual revenge until Isaac died.

The word *hated* can be translated "bore a grudge." The same word is found in Genesis 50:15. In this respect, Esau's inward rage against Jacob was like that of Cain against Abel (Gen. 4:5–8).

2. Rebekah's actions (27:42–46)

As soon as Rebekah became aware of this danger to Jacob, she acted quickly. She did two things. She called in Jacob and told him to go to the house of her brother Laban and to stay until Esau was willing to set aside his anger (27:42–45). She went to Isaac and told him that he ought to send Jacob to Haran to get a wife rather than choosing a Canaanite as a wife (27:46).

3. Isaac's instructions and blessing (28:1–5)

Isaac, therefore, told Jacob not to take a Canaanite wife but to go to the house of Bethuel, Rebekah's father, in order to find a wife from the daughters of Laban (28:1–2). Isaac then asked God to bless Jacob with the blessing of Abraham—many descendants and the land (28:3–4). Thus did Jacob set forth on his journey (28:5).

4. Esau's marriages (28:6–9)

Esau was aware of all this (28:6–7). Esau had already married some Hittite women, an act that displeased his parents (28:8; see 26:34–35). Esau went to Ishmael's family and married one of Ishmael's daughters (28:9).

II. Jacob's Encounter with God (Gen. 28:10–22)

1. Jacob's crisis (28:10–11)

10 And Jacob went out from Beer-sheba, and went toward Haran.

11 And lighted upon a certain place, and tarried there all night, because the sun was set; and he took one of the stones of that place, and put them for his pillows, and lay down in that place to sleep.

Beersheba was where Jacob had been living within the household of his father. He set out for Haran, the place from which Abraham had journeyed when he first came to Canaan (Gen. 12:5). Haran was also the place where Abraham had sent his servant to find a wife for Isaac. Haran was where Rebekah had grown up and where her father, brother, and nieces lived. Genesis 24:10 calls it "the city of Nahor," Abraham's brother and Rebekah's grandfather. Haran was also sometimes called Padan-Aram (Gen. 28:6). It was a journey of several hundred miles. When Abraham and Rebekah came over his caravan route, they had others with them; but Jacob was alone. He also must have been homesick, especially for his mother, who had always watched out for him.

2. God's revelation (28:12–15)

12 And he dreamed, and behold a ladder set up on the earth, and the top of it reached to heaven: and behold the angels of God ascending and descending on it.

13 And, behold, the LORD stood above it, and said, I am the LORD God of Abraham thy father, and the God of Isaac: the land whereon thou liest, to thee will I give it, and to thy seed;

14 And thy seed shall be as the dust of the earth, and thou shalt spread abroad to the west, and to the east, and to the north, and to the south: and in thee and in thy seed shall all the families of the earth be blessed.

15 And behold, I am with thee, and will keep thee in all places whither thou goest, and will bring thee again into this land; for I will not leave thee, until I have done that which I have spoken to thee of.

During Bible times, God often revealed Himself through dreams. Jacob was one of the first to receive a revelation of God in a dream vision. Jacob saw a stairway to heaven. Angels were going up and coming down on it. Above it was God. The "ladder" was not what we call a ladder so much as stairs. The angels apparently carried human prayers and needs up to heaven and returned with answers and help. The help came from God, who now spoke to Jacob.

God revealed Himself as the Lord, using the personal name of the God of the Hebrews. He was the God of Abraham and of Isaac. Abraham was actually Jacob's grandfather, but he was his "father" in the sense of forefather. The miracle is that God used the words *thou, thee,* and *thy* to show that He was extending to Jacob the blessing and promises to Abraham and Isaac. He had been the God of Abraham and Isaac; now He declared Himself also the God of Jacob. This was an act of sheer grace because Jacob surely had done nothing to deserve God's favor and choice. To the contrary, he had acted in ways that would seem to disqualify him as the father of the chosen people of God.

The Lord repeated the aspects of the blessing that He had given to Abraham and to Isaac. The blessing included the land, many descendants, and becoming a channel of blessing to all people. This is the fifth time that this emphasis on the worldwide purpose of God was stated in the story of God's dealings with the patriarchs (12:3; 18:18; 22:18; 26:4).

God made three other promises directly to Jacob in his current crisis. God promised to be with him, to keep him, and to bring him back to his homeland. God promised His presence, provision for what lay ahead, and hope for the final outcome. All three of these promises were needed by Jacob as he faced an unknown future. These promises are typical promises to people of faith. Psalm 23, for example, is the testimony of one who trusted God's love and care and claimed the promise of His presence while in the presence of enemies and while passing through the valley of the shadow.

3. Jacob's initial responses (28:16–19)

16 And Jacob awaked out of his sleep, and he said, Surely the LORD is in this place; and I knew it not.

18 And Jacob rose up early in the morning, and took the stone that he had put for his pillows, and set it up for a pillar, and poured oil upon the top of it.

19 And he called the name of that place Beth-el: but the name of that city was called Luz at the first.

What feelings were expressed by Jacob in the words of verse 16? Surely one feeling was surprise. He admitted that he had been unaware that the Lord was in that place. This may mean that Jacob associated God only with Beersheba, where his believing father lived. It may imply that Jacob was surprised to encounter God anywhere. As far as the Bible tells us, God had never revealed Himself to Jacob before; nor had Jacob tried to contact God.

Perhaps mixed with Jacob's surprise were feelings of remorse for his past sins, especially for ignoring his need for a personal encounter with God. Verse 17 says that Jacob also had a sense of awe when he recognized that the Lord had appeared to him and spoken to him. Suddenly he realized that the stairway to heaven was like the very gate into the presence of the holy God.

Jacob put his feelings into actions. First, he set up one of the large stones as a pillar to mark the spot of his encounter with God. Such pillars were used as religious memorials. Oil was used to consecrate the stone. Jacob built no altar at this time, perhaps because God had already spoken to him. Years later, when he and his family came to Bethel, he built an altar (Gen. 35:3).

He named the place Bethel. *El* was the shortened form for the word for God, and *beth* meant "house." The name is one of several indications that Jacob had come to a time of personal faith in God.

4. Jacob's vow (28:20–22)

20 And Jacob vowed a vow, saying, If God will be with me, and will keep me in the way that I go, and will give me bread to eat, and raiment to put on,

21 So that I come again to my father's house in peace; then shall the LORD be my God:

22 And this stone, which I have set for a pillar, shall be God's house: and of all that thou shalt give me I will surely give the tenth unto thee.

Jacob's vow is a subject of debate. Some feel that his vow was a crude attempt by Jacob, the shrewd dealer, to make a bargain with God. According to his view, Jacob offered someday to make the Lord his God only if and when God kept all His promises to Jacob. Other Bible students, however, disagree with this interpretation of Jacob's vow. The latter group makes the following points:

1. The passage can be translated by moving "then" in verse 21 to verse 22, thus making the last part of verse 21 one of the promises of God that Jacob was affirming. To paraphrase this view, Jacob said if God would be with him, provide for his needs, return him to his homeland, and be his God, *then* he would express his gratitude by returning to Bethel to worship and by giving God a tithe.

2. Even if the usual translation is correct, such a vow was more than a crude bargain that reflected lack of faith by Jacob. The vow did not ask for anything God had not promised; therefore, it was a way of Jacob showing that he accepted these promises by faith.

3. Also remember that God accepts initial expressions of faith as long as they are sincere. Jacob probably did not know any other way of relating to others than by bargaining. If he used similar terms in his first encounter with God, God accepted Jacob as he was. After all, this was Jacob's first expression of faith. He later expressed his faith in more mature ways.

Abraham had given a tithe to Melchizedek (Gen. 14:20). Jacob promised to do the same. Tithing was and is a way of signifying that all we have belongs to God. At some point in these events, the God of his father and grandfather had become his God. In order for faith to be real, it must be personal.

SUMMARY OF BIBLE TRUTHS

1. Times of crisis often set the stage for encounters with God.
2. God offers Himself to sinners as an act of sheer grace.
3. God promises to be with us, care for us, and lead us home.
4. People often are surprised by God.
5. God accepts sincere expressions of initial faith, even if they are immature.
6. Real faith involves a personal relationship with God.

APPLYING THE BIBLE

1. A critical decision. I received a call thirty minutes ago reporting the death of a man in our town. Four days ago I heard of his worsening condition and that he might have only a few days to live because of the ravages of cancer. I went to the hospital that night and sat and talked with him about his relationship with the Lord. It was the first time I had ever had that opportunity and, even though I knew his wife and children professed Christ, I was not sure about where he stood with the Lord. In the course of that conversation, he indicated a rich church tradition, having served as a lad in several church positions, but he manifested serious uncertainty as to whether he had ever met the Lord personally. I asked him if he would like to settle the issue forever, to ask the Lord into his life and to have the assurance of a personal relationship with Him. He said he would, and joyously invited Christ to come into his life. About fifty-five hours later, he died!

Suddenly, all the man's other acquaintances, which are many, mean nothing in the light of his acquaintance with God! Jacob knew the same about his personal faith-response to God. And so must every person.

An interesting footnote about that experience: Upon leaving for that hospital visit, I told a custodian about it and asked him to pray for the dying man, that he would receive Christ. The custodian, a new and uninstructed Christian, said, "Pastor, if he dies before you get there, can he go to heaven? Isn't there some way you can join him up to God even if he's already dead?" The Bible is explicit: A person must be "joined up" to God before death to go to heaven.

2. About God meeting man:

▶ Alan Seeger once wrote a poem entitled: "I Have a Rendezvous with Death." That is why it is so important, before that certain rendezvous, that we have a rendezvous with God!

▶ "God is always laying His benevolent ambush for somebody" (Anonymous).

▶ "God enters into every man's soul by a private entrance" (Anonymous).

Robert Browning wrote the following lines in "Bishop Bloughram's Apology":

> Just when we are safest (from God),
> there's a sunset-touch,
> A fancy from a flower-bell, some one's death,
> A chorus-ending from Euripides.

3. Tithing before Moses. Jacob's pledge to tithe is instructing. Since time immemorial, men have given at least a tithe of their income to God. That was true long before Moses wrote down the law requiring tithing. (The theory is that primitive men settled on a tenth because they knew men's hands were required to provide a living, so they gave a tenth representing one of man's fingers, a part of his productive power.)

4. For Discussion:

▶ Do you think Jacob was taught by his parents to tithe?

▶ Is it proper to teach your child to tithe before he or she becomes a Christian?

▶ Is it possible for a person to truly know and follow God without some tangible, monetary expression of his or her faith?

▶ Should a Christian give at least a tithe of his income to the Lord? On what basis?

5. On meeting God.

▶ Can you think of a time in your life's journey when you were surprised by God?

▶ Would you have known it was God unless, by His Spirit, that fact had been revealed to you?

▶ How would you have interpreted the event if God had not made you aware it was Him?

▶ Is God attempting to speak to people today? (See Titus 2:11, "For the grace of God that bringeth salvation hath appeared to all men." And Acts 14:17, "He [God] hath not left himself without witness.")

▶ How can we prepare ourselves to hear the voice of God?

6. God's gift of grace. John Stott has written, "The repeated promises in the Qur'an (Koran) of the forgiveness of a compassionate and merciful Allah are all made to the meritorious, whose merits have been weighed in Allah's scales, whereas the gospel is good news of mercy to the undeserving. The symbol of the religion of Jesus is the cross, not the scales."[1]

7. Redemptive results. God sovereignly weaves the patterns of our lives into redemptive results. When the Persians are making a carpet, they "put it up vertically on a frame, and they have little boys sitting on various levels on the rug, on the wrong side. The artist stands on the right side of the rug, the side on which people will tread, and he shouts his instructions to the boys on the other side. Sometimes a boy will make a mistake on the rug. I have a Persian rug in my possession, given me by an Arab sheikh whose guest I was for some time in Mesopotamia. The pattern of the rug suddenly develops a yellow irregularity. Ineed, such asymmetry in design is a mark that a Persian rug was made in Persia and not in Wolverhampton! I said to the student, 'What happens when the boy makes a mistake?' 'Well,' he said, 'quite often the artist does not make the little boy take out the wrong colour. If the artist is a great enough artist he weaves the mistake into the pattern.'"[2]

TEACHING THE BIBLE

▶ *Main Idea:* Jacob's flight and vision enabled him to develop a personal relationship with God.
▶ *Suggested Teaching Aim:* To lead adults to identify steps they can take to deepen their relationship with God.

A TEACHING OUTLINE

Jacob's Flight and Vision

1. *Jacob's Flight (Gen. 27:41–28:9)*
2. *Jacob's Encounter with God (Gen. 28:10–22)*

Introduce the Bible Study

Ask members to listen for references to Jacob's experience at Bethel as you read the words to "Nearer, My God, to Thee." (Do not use 1991 *The Baptist Hymnal;* it does not have all the stanzas.) Say, Today's lesson will help us examine God's revelation to Jacob at Bethel and help us analyze Jacob's responses.

Search for Biblical Truth

IN ADVANCE, enlist a reader to read the Focal Passages when called on. Plan to combine lecture and a study guide to present the lesson material. Prepare and distribute the following study guide to each member (without italicized answers). (If you choose not to distribute study guides, you can use these questions as a group discussion guide.)

Study Guide

1. Who was Jacob's brother? *(Esau.)*
2. Why had the brother decided to kill Jacob? *(Jacob had cheated him out of the birthright and blessing.)*
3. Why was Jacob on his way to Haran? *(Primarily to get away from Esau; also to find a wife from his mother's people.)*
4. How far was it from Beersheba to Haran? *(Several hundred miles.)*

PAGE
71

5. What did Jacob see in his dream? *(Angels ascending and descending stairs to heaven.)*
6. How did God identify Himself? *(God of Abraham and Jacob.)*
7. What did God promise him? *(Prosperity and protection.)*
8. What was Jacob's response when he woke? *(Amazement; he set up a stone pillar and called the place "House of God" or Bethel.)*
9. Describe Jacob's vow. *(He bargained that if God would protect him he would make him his God—but see "Studying the Bible" for other viewpoints.)*
10. What had Jacob done to earn God's blessings? *(Nothing)*

After the reader has read 27:41, lecture on questions 1–4. Use a map of Old Testament times to locate Beersheba, Haran, and Bethel or Luz. Ask members to answer questions 1–4.

After the reader has read 28:10–15, lecture on questions 5–7. Ask members to answer questions 5–7.

After the reader has read 28:16–19, lecture on question 8. Ask members to answer question 8.

After the reader has read 28:20–22, lecture on questions 9–10. Ask members to answer questions 9–10.

Give the Truth a Personal Focus

Read "Nearer, My God, to Thee" again. Ask members if they can understand more references to Jacob's experience at Bethel.

IN ADVANCE, write the six statements in "Summary of Bible Truths" on small slips of paper. Distribute these to six groups. (If your class has fewer than six members, select those statements you think would apply best to your members' needs.) Ask the groups, based on their statement, to identify steps they can take to deepen their relationship with God. (For example, based on the first statement, members might say something like, "We can look for what God is saying to us in the midst of our crises.")

As members suggest steps, write these on a chalkboard or a large sheet of paper. Ask members to look at the completed list and to choose one specific step they will agree to begin work on this coming week. Close in a prayer of commitment.

---

1. John R. W. Stott in *Christianity Today,* January 6, 1979, p. 53.
2. Leslie Weatherhead, *Why Do Men Suffer?* (London: SCM Press, 1935), 150–151.

Jacob's Struggle at Peniel

Background Passage: Genesis 32:3–33:17
Focal Passages: Genesis 32:9–11, 24–30; 33:1–4

When Jacob left Canaan because of Esau's plan to kill him, God revealed Himself to Jacob at Bethel. When Jacob returned to Canaan after twenty years in Haran, he had another significant encounter with God at Peniel. This was probably the watershed experience in Jacob's spiritual pilgrimage.

▶**Study Aim:** *To describe what happened when Jacob returned to Canaan and to explain its significance for his spiritual pilgrimage.*

STUDYING THE BIBLE

OUTLINE AND SUMMARY

   I. **Meeting God (Gen. 32:3–32)**
      1. **Fear of Esau (32:3–8)**
      2. **Jacob's prayer (32:9–12)**
      3. **Further preparations to meet Esau (32:13–21)**
      4. **Wrestling with God (32:22–32)**
  II. **Meeting Esau (Gen. 33:1–17)**
      1. **Last-minute preparations (33:1–3)**
      2. **Welcomed by Esau (33:4–11)**
      3. **Going their separate ways (33:12–17)**

When Jacob returned to Canaan, he feared what Esau might do (32:3–8). Jacob prayed (32:9–12). He sent a series of gifts to Esau (32:13–21). That night Jacob had a wrestling match that he called an encounter with God (32:22–32). As Esau approached, Jacob put Rachel and Joseph in the safest place (33:1–3). Esau welcomed Jacob warmly (33:4–11). Then the brothers went their separate ways (33:12–17).

I. Meeting God (Gen. 32:3–32)
1. Fear of Esau (32:3–8)

As Jacob approached Canaan, he sent messengers to Edom to tell Esau of Jacob's prosperity from his years with Laban. Jacob's message also asked that he might find favor with Esau (32:3–5). Jacob's messengers returned with word that Esau was coming to meet Jacob, and that Esau had with him four hundred men (32:6). In light of Esau's threats of twenty years earlier (27:41), Jacob was terrified at what Esau intended to do. Jacob divided his company so that if Esau attacked one part, the other might escape (32:7–8).

2. Jacob's prayer (32:9–12)

     9 And Jacob said, O God of my father Abraham, and God of my father Isaac, the LORD which saidst unto me, Return

unto thy country, and to thy kindred, and I will deal well with thee;

10 I am not worthy of the least of all the mercies, and of all the truth, which thou hast shewed unto thy servant; for with my staff I passed over this Jordan; and now I am become two bands.

11 Deliver me, I pray thee, from the hand of my brother, from the hand of Esau: for I fear him, lest he will come and smite me, and the mother with the children.

Jacob had spent the last twenty years in Haran, working for Laban, Rebekah's brother. During those years, Jacob married, raised a family, and carried on a constant struggle with Laban, who was as wily and tricky as Jacob himself had ever been. Little is said during those years about any growth in Jacob's faith. In his final complaint to Laban about how Laban had mistreated him, Jacob acknowledged that God had blessed him in spite of all Laban's efforts (31:36–42). Thus, Genesis 32:9–12 is only the second time in Genesis where we hear Jacob addressing God.

He called on the God of Abraham and Isaac, with no mention of Him also being the God of Jacob. This, of course, is not proof that Jacob did not have personal faith; however, it fits the picture of a busy man who had allowed his faith to remain largely inactive. Therefore, the fact that Jacob prayed at all is worth noting. Jacob was by nature a man who liked to be in control. He believed that God helps those who help themselves. This character trait had enabled him to hold his own against Laban, who had a temperament much like Jacob's.

After twenty years in Haran, the Lord had told Jacob to return to Canaan (31:13). When God had revealed Himself to Jacob at the beginning of his trip to Haran, God promised to be with Jacob, to keep him, and to bring him back to Canaan (28:15). Jacob reminded the Lord of His command for Jacob to return and of His promise to care for him.

Verse 10 is one of the most memorable prayers in the Bible. It certainly represented a high point in Jacob's prayer life. Jacob expressed gratitude, trust, and humility. God had indeed blessed Jacob. He had left home with only his staff; he returned with servants and livestock. He had become a wealthy man in spite of all Laban's efforts. Jacob acknowledged that he was not worthy of any of these blessings. All of God's blessings had been gifts of pure grace, none of which Jacob deserved. For a man like Jacob to recognize and acknowledge this truth to himself and God was an encouraging sign of Jacob's spiritual potential.

Verse 11 was Jacob's earnest prayer to be delivered and protected from whatever harm Esau might do to him or his family. He had taken steps to try to appease Esau, and he would soon take other steps. However, Jacob was beginning to realize that this was a situation beyond his control. He could do all he could to appease Esau, but that might not be enough. Jacob's life was in the hands of God. It always had been, but Jacob was just learning that lesson.

Verse 12—like verse 10—claimed God's earlier promises to fulfill His purposes through Jacob and his descendants.

3. Further preparations to meet Esau (32:13–21)

Although it was night by now, Jacob was still coming up with strategies to appease Esau. He sent a series of presents to Esau with a message that these were presents from his servant Jacob to his lord Esau.

4. Wrestling with God (32:22–32)

> **24** And Jacob was left alone; and there wrestled a man with him until the breaking of the day.
>
> **25** And when he saw that he prevailed not against him, he touched the hollow of his thigh; and the hollow of Jacob's thigh was out of joint, as he wrestled with him.
>
> **26** And he said, Let me go, for the day breaketh. And he said, I will not let thee go, except thou bless me.
>
> **27** And he said unto him, What is thy name? And he said, Jacob.
>
> **28** And he said, Thy name shall be called no more Jacob, but Israel: for as a prince hast thou power with God and with men, and hast prevailed.
>
> **29** And Jacob asked him, and said, Tell me, I pray thee, thy name. And he said, Wherefore is it that thou dost ask after my name? And he blessed him there.
>
> **30** And Jacob called the name of the place Peniel: for I have seen God face to face, and my life is preserved.

This strange incident took place while Jacob was alone during that same long night. He had done all he knew to do, even sending his family across the ford Jabbok (32:22–23). Now he lingered alone in the darkness, wondering if there was anything he had overlooked and wondering if God had heard his prayer. As yet, he had received no response from the Lord. Then suddenly a man grabbed him and began to wrestle with him.

This incident has always challenged Bible students. It raises some questions that are hard to answer, but it contains some truths that are worth digging out. The first question is, "Who was the man with whom Jacob wrestled?" Jacob may not have known when the man suddenly loomed out of the darkness and grabbed him. However, at some point, Jacob came to believe that the man was God; for he named the place "the face of God."

Another tough question is, "Why did the Lord initiate a wrestling match with Jacob?" Closely related is the question, "Why did the Lord allow Jacob to hold his own in this match?" The Lord could have easily won the match; however, He seems to have been testing Jacob's faith and desire for God and His blessing. Jacob's persistence and his refusal to let go even though crippled show his awareness of the depth of his need for God's help and blessing.

"Why did each ask the other his name?" God surely knew who Jacob was, but he gave Jacob an opportunity to say the name that reminded him of his past actions as "supplanter." This in turn gave God the opportunity to give Jacob a new name "Israel." The name means "God prevails." In the past, Jacob had often lived as if everything depended on Jacob prevailing by various means. Now he was given a name that reminded him and others that the real source of any prevailing on his part came from God.

Jacob asked his opponent who he was because he had begun to suspect that He was God. God's refusal to tell His name shows that God does not fully unveil Himself whenever someone asks. This also explains why the Lord did not want Jacob to hold Him until the sun rose. Although Jacob later said that he had seen God face to face, this was an overstatement. He wrestled with God in the darkness. He never saw God's full glory; if he had, he would have been overwhelmed by it.

"Who won this wrestling match?" This seems to have been the ultimate "win-win" situation. In a sense, both seemed to lose. God seemed to have been unable to break away from Jacob's hold and thus was forced to bless him. Jacob went away crippled by a powerful blow. However, God wanted Jacob to continue to cling to Him as he did; and Jacob, although crippled during the struggle, emerged with the blessing he had sought. When the sun rose, his opponent was gone; and Jacob limped off to meet Esau (32:31–32).

II. Meeting Esau (Gen. 33:1–17)

1. Last-minute preparations (33:1–3)

1 And Jacob lifted up his eyes, and looked, and behold Esau came, and with him four hundred men. And he divided the children unto Leah, and unto Rachel, and unto the two handmaids.

2 And he put the handmaids and their children foremost, and Leah and her children after, and Rachel and Joseph hindermost.

3 And he passed over before them, and bowed himself to the ground seven times, until he came near to his brother.

As Jacob made his way back to his family, he saw Esau and men approaching. They were still far enough away for Jacob to make one last-minute precaution. He divided his family into three groups. He placed at the front of his family the two maids Bilhah and Zilpah; each had borne two sons for Jacob and their respective mistresses. Next Jacob placed Leah and her six sons and one daughter. Last of all he placed his favorite Rachel and her son Joseph.

At least Jacob had the faith and courage to take the point. If an attack came, he no doubt would receive the first blows. As he and Esau moved toward one another, Jacob still had no clue what his brother intended to do. Jacob, therefore, approached Esau by humbly bowing seven times—an accepted sign of submission to a superior.

2. Welcomed by Esau (33:4)

4 And Esau ran to meet him, and embraced him, and fell on his neck, and kissed him, and they wept.

This was Esau's finest hour. He welcomed his deceitful brother with open arms and with genuine joy. The wording of Esau's joyful welcome of Jacob reminds us of Jesus' description of how the father welcomed home his prodigal son (Luke 15:20). Jacob also joined in the weeping, no doubt shedding tears of relief and gratitude.

How can we explain the remarkable change in Esau's attitude? Esau may have been impressed by Jacob's obvious desire to be welcomed, not attacked. Although Jacob never actually confessed to any past wrongdoing, his present actions perhaps implied it to Esau. At any rate, Esau welcomed him; and they were reconciled. When Esau asked about the women and children, Jacob introduced his family as each group passed by and bowed to Esau (33:5–7). When Esau asked about the presents Jacob had sent ahead to him, Jacob said these were gifts (33:8). When Esau protested that he had plenty of his own, Jacob urged his brother to accept his gifts, which Esau finally agreed to do (33:9–11).

3. Going their separate ways (33:12–17)

Esau asked Jacob to go with him and his men, but Jacob declined because women and children would needlessly slow down mounted men (33:12–14). Esau offered to provide an escort, but Jacob said that they didn't need one (33:15). Thus they went their separate ways: Esau back to Mount Seir, and Jacob to Succoth.

SUMMARY OF BIBLE TRUTHS

1. Life's crises provide opportunities for spiritual renewal.
2. None of us is worthy of the least of God's blessings.
3. Prayer expresses our gratitude and trust.
4. God sometimes confronts us in unexpected ways.
5. God sometimes tests our perseverance.
6. Reconciliation with family is crucial.

APPLYING THE BIBLE

1. Evidence of change. A deacon once served in a church I was pastoring who could prove his genuine conversion, he said, by the fact that just after receiving Christ—as a middle-aged adult—he saw a man with black skin and didn't hate him. He said he'd never had that experience before and knew only God could have done it. Furthermore, he never reverted to his former racist beliefs or feelings. Jacob's walk—after meeting God—was forever different. His name was changed and his walk was changed.

Note that the difference in Jacob's walk was public; everybody who knew him saw it. He who professes to have met God and manifests no public evidence of it has not met God!

For discussion: Will a meeting with God automatically affect one's outward behaviour? Specifically, what marked changes may we expect to see in the lives of those who have met God? What other changes have you observed in your own life, or others, because of an encounter with God? Will all the changes that God has planned for our lives show up immediately after conversion?

2. The testing time. The Chinese word for "crisis" means "dangerous opportunity." We speak, today, of a "defining moment" or of "the pedagogical moment" (the moment at which we are truly prepared to learn something). For Jacob, Peniel was all that and more! Discuss the following questions:

▶ How do we prepare for such moments?
▶ Do we always have forewarning of them?

4. Jacob's two tests. Jacob faced two tests: meeting his brother and meeting God. He passed both tests. (Remember that God had told him that he would have power with God and man; that was true because he did pass those two tests.) Name some of the possible results if Jacob had failed either or both of those tests.

5. Persistence. Jacob was persistent in his pursuit of God's blessings that night. E. M. Bounds says, "Our laziness after God is our crying sin."And Calvin Coolidge once said: "Press on. Nothing can take the place of persistence. Talent will not. Nothing is more common than unsuccessful men with talent. Genius will not. Unrewarded genius is almost a proverb. Education will not. The world is full of educated derelicts. Persistence and determination alone are overwhelmingly powerful."

6. God's mercies. Jacob expressed heartfelt gratitude to God for His mercies in Genesis 32:10. I saw these lines somewhere years ago:

> One midnight deep in starlight still,
> I dreamed that I received this bill—
> 5,000 breathless dawns all new;
> 5,000 flowers, fresh with dew;
> 5,000 sunsets, wrapped in gold;
> 1,000,000 snowflakes served ice cold;
> 5 quiet friends, one baby's love;
> 100 music-haunted dreams, moon-drenched
> roads and hurrying streams;
> A prophesying wind, and trees;
> A silent star and browsing bees;
> One June night in the fragrant woods;
> One heart that loved and understood.
> I wondered when I waked that day,
> How—how in God's name—I could pay.

TEACHING THE BIBLE

▶ *Main Idea:* Jacob's struggle at Peniel was a high spiritual moment for him.
▶ *Suggested Teaching Aim:* To lead adults to identify high spiritual moments in their spiritual pilgrimages.

A TEACHING OUTLINE

Jacob's Struggle at Peniel (Gen. 32:3–33:17)

1. *Meeting God (32:3–32)*
2. *Meeting Esau (33:1–17)*

Introduce the Bible Study

Use #1 from "Applying the Bible" to introduce the Bible study. Point out that Jacob's experience at Peniel affected him as nothing had before.

Search for Biblical Truth

IN ADVANCE, write the following headings on four large strips of paper; write the questions (omit italicized answers) on the back of each strip. Tape the strips to the backs of four chairs. Ask the person with strip number 1 to read the Scripture and ask the questions. Let members respond. Place the strip on the focal wall when all the questions have been asked. Follow this procedure for all four strips. If you choose not to write these out, you can use them as a basis for a group discussion.

I. Jacob's Prayer (Gen. 32:9–12)
1. Where had Jacob been for the past twenty years of his life? *(In Haran at his uncle Laban's.)*
2. Why was Jacob so worried at this point? *(He was at Peniel and would come face to face with Esau tomorrow.)*
3. What in Jacob's prayer indicated that some spiritual growth had taken place in the intervening years? *("I am not worthy.")*
4. What indicated that he still did not trust God completely? *(He still feared Esau.)*

II. Wrestling with God (Gen 32:22–32)
1. Who was the man with whom Jacob wrestled? *(Jacob believed he was God.)*
2. Why did the man and Jacob each ask the other's name? *(Asking Jacob's name gave God a chance to give Jacob a new name, Israel; Jacob suspected his opponent was God.)*
3. Who won this wrestling match? *(Both; Jacob got a new name and God got Jacob to cling to Him.)*

III. Last-minute Preparations (Gen. 33:1–3)
1. What shows that Jacob did not trust God completely to deliver him from Esau? *(He still plotted to arrange his family so they could escape.)*
2. Where did Jacob position himself? *(In the front—the most dangerous place.)*

IV. Welcomed by Esau (Gen. 33:4)
1. How did Esau respond to Jacob? *(With open arms.)*
2. What had caused Esau's feelings toward Jacob to change?

Give the Truth a Personal Focus

Distribute paper and pencils to members. **IN ADVANCE,** copy on a large sheet of paper the six statements in "Summary of Bible Truths." Display these statements and read them aloud to the class. Ask members to choose one of these statements and write a paragraph to describe how this statement could help them have a high spiritual experience in their Christian pilgrimage.

As an alternate idea, if you choose not to do this individually, you can use the six statements to lead a group discussion with the whole class or organize members into six groups of one or more persons and assign each group one of the statements.

From Favored Son to Slave

Background Passage: Genesis 37:1–35
Focal Passages: Genesis 37:3–4,17b–28

Each of the four main personalities in Genesis 12–50 was different, but God used each to further His plan. The role of Joseph was to be the preserver of his family from starvation. God in His providence worked to achieve this good purpose even though Joseph's brothers sold him as a slave.

▶**Study Aim:** *To describe and analyze the actions of Jacob, Joseph, Reuben, Judah, and the other brothers.*

STUDYING THE BIBLE

OUTLINE AND SUMMARY

   I. **The Hatred of Joseph's Brothers (Gen. 37:1–11)**
       1. **Joseph's evil report on his brothers (37:1–2)**
       2. **Israel's favoritism toward Joseph (37:3–4)**
       3. **Joseph's dreams (37:5–11)**
   II. **The Evil Actions of Joseph's Brothers (Gen. 37:12–35)**
       1. **Joseph's mission to find and report (37:12–17)**
       2. **Plan 1: kill Joseph (37:18–20)**
       3. **Plan 2: put Joseph in a pit (37:21–24)**
       4. **Plan 3: sell Joseph (37:25–28)**
       5. **Plan 4: cover up (37:29–32)**
       6. **Jacob's grief (37:33–35)**

Joseph's brothers hated him for reporting their sins (37:1–2), being his father's favorite (37:3–4), and telling them his dreams (37:5–12). Israel sent Joseph to find his brothers and the flocks (37:12–17). The brothers saw him and conspired to kill him (37:18–20). Reuben persuaded them to put him in a pit instead (37:21–24). Judah persuaded the others to sell Joseph, rather than kill him (37:25–28). The brothers put blood on Joseph's coat and took it to Jacob (37:29–32). Jacob went into deep mourning (37:33–35).

I. The Hatred of Joseph's Brothers (Gen. 37:1–11)

1. Joseph's evil report on his brothers (37:1–2)

Verse 2 describes the first of three reasons why Joseph's brothers hated him—he told his father Jacob (Israel) the bad things that four of his brothers did. These were the sons of Bilhah, Dan, and Naphtali, and the sons of Zilpah, Zebulun, and Asher. We also learn that Joseph was seventeen years old and was a shepherd like the rest of his family.

2. Israel's favoritism toward Joseph (37:3–4)

3 Now Israel loved Joseph more than all his children, because he was the son of his old age: and he made him a coat of many colours.

4 And when his brethren saw that their father loved him more than all his brethren, they hated him, and could not speak peaceably unto him.

A key factor in the hatred of the brothers toward Joseph was Israel's obvious favoritism toward Joseph. (Notice that Jacob is called by his new name—Israel—throughout most of Gen. 37.) He loved Joseph more than any of the others; in fact, verse 3 may mean that he loved him more than all the rest put together. After all, Rachel was Israel's favorite wife. And Joseph was the only son of Rachel. Rachel later died giving birth to Benjamin. Thus, later, Benjamin was more the son of Israel's old age than Joseph; however, at the time of Genesis 37, Joseph was the youngest of his sons.

Israel made an open display of his greater love for Joseph by giving him a special coat. Translators debate the appearance of the coat. Was it primarily characterized by its many colors, or was it primarily a coat with long sleeves? No one disagrees about the purpose of the coat. It not only showed Israel's greater love for Joseph, but it also set Joseph apart as more important than the rest. That was truly a time when clothes made the man, and special clothing was a real mark of honor.

There is also no debate about the effect this had on the brothers of Joseph. Leah's six sons joined the other four in hating Joseph for his place of special favor with their father. No doubt they all remembered how Jacob had placed their lives at risk and protected Joseph when Esau approached (33:1–2). The coat was the final straw for them. The word translated "hated" means more than an attitude; it refers to an act. Their hatred was an evil act just waiting to happen.

The brothers hated Joseph so much that they could not hide it. They were unable to act and speak normally when Joseph was around. Their words were words that showed their inner rage.

3. Joseph's dreams (37:5–11)

Then to make matters worse, there were Joseph's dreams, which he freely told to his family. The dreams showed Joseph in a position of honor over his family. The brothers hated him for his dreams (37:5). His dream of their sheaves of grain bowing to his sheaf made them hate him (37:6–8). His dream of sun, moon, and eleven stars bowing to him even caused his father to rebuke Joseph (37:9–10). The brothers envied him all the more, and his father began to wonder about such dreams (37:11).

II. The Evil Actions of Joseph's Brothers (Gen. 37:12–35)

1. Joseph's mission to find and report (37:12–17)

17 And Joseph went after his brethren, and found them in Dothan.

The brothers were with their father's flock in Shechem (37:12). Jacob sent Joseph to find them and ensure that all was well. He was to report back to his father (37:13–14). By the time Joseph reached Shechem, the brothers had moved to another location. A man found Joseph wandering the fields and asked what he sought (37:15). When Joseph explained that he was looking for his brothers, the man told him that they had moved to Dothan, about fifteen miles north of Shechem (37:16–17). That is where Joseph found them.

2. Plan 1: kill Joseph (37:18–20)

18 And when they saw him afar off, even before he came near unto them, they conspired against him to slay him.

19 And they said one to another, Behold, this dreamer cometh.

20 Come now therefore, and let us slay him, and cast him into some pit, and we will say, Some evil beast hath devoured him: and we shall see what will become of his dreams.

The hatred of the brothers now developed into a plan of action. When they saw Joseph in the distance, they probably recognized his despised coat first of all, They conspired to kill their brother. They referred to him sarcastically as "the dreamer." They proposed to kill Joseph and throw his body into a pit. Then they would report to Jacob that Joseph had been killed by a wild animal.

Joseph's dreams were a source of their anger. Not only did they call him the dreamer, but they also intended to make sure that Joseph's grand dreams never came true. The surest way to do that was to kill the dreamer and thus his dreams. Like Cain and Esau, their hatred of their brother caused them to plan to take his life.

3. Plan 2: put Joseph in a pit (37:21–24)

21 And Reuben heard it, and he delivered him out of their hands; and said, Let us not kill him.

22 And Reuben said unto them, Shed no blood, but cast him into this pit that is in the wilderness, and lay no hand upon him; that he might rid him out of their hands, to deliver him to his father again.

23 And it came to pass, when Joseph was come unto his brethren, that they stripped Joseph out of his coat, his coat of many colours that was on him.

24 And they took him, and cast him into a pit: and the pit was empty, there was no water in it.

The statement that Reuben "heard" them shows that not all the brothers were part of the initial conspiracy to kill Joseph. Reuben was the oldest of Jacob's children; therefore, Jacob expected him to act responsibly. Reuben, therefore, accepted this responsibility and tried to save Joseph's life. His plan was to talk the others out of killing Joseph and instead throw him into a pit. A key feature of Reuben's plan was to rescue Joseph from the pit and take him home safely to his father.

Thus, Reuben appealed to the others not to become guilty of shedding blood. Although at times the brothers had been quick to shed the blood of others (Gen. 34), shedding the blood of one's brother was particularly heinous. No doubt the brothers knew the story of what God told Cain about the blood of his brother crying out to God for vengeance (Gen. 4:10). Jacob probably also had taught them what God said to Noah and all humanity about taking human life (Gen. 9:6).

Reuben was successful in persuading the others not to kill Joseph. They threw Joseph into a pit that was empty and contained no water. Genesis 37 does not tell us what Joseph was saying and doing during all this time. However, when the brothers later were arguing about their evil actions, they recalled how Joseph had pleaded with them and how they had ignored him (Gen. 42:21).

4. Plan 3: sell Joseph (37:25–28)

> **25 And they sat down to eat bread: and they lifted up their eyes and looked, and behold, a company of Ishmeelites came from Gilead with their camels bearing spicery and balm and myrrh, going to carry it down to Egypt.**
>
> **26 And Judah said unto his brethren, What profit is it if we slay our brother, and conceal his blood?**
>
> **27 Come, and let us sell him to the Ishmeelites, and let not our hand be upon him; for he is our brother and our flesh. And his brethren were content.**

After throwing their brother into a pit, the brothers showed how callous they were by sitting down and eating. While they were eating, they saw a caravan approaching. Judah then proposed that they sell their brother rather than kill him. He gave two reasons. For one thing, if they killed him, they would have nothing to show for it. If they sold him, they would have some money. Second, Judah emphasized—even more than Reuben—the terrible crime of shedding the blood of their own brother. He said that they did not want Joseph's blood on their hands. After all, although they hated him, he was their brother—their own flesh and blood.

We cannot tell what Judah's motives were. The best view of his motives assumes that he acted like Reuben primarily to save Joseph's life. Later he showed this kind of nobility of spirit (Gen. 44:18–34), but we don't know if he was that kind of person on the night they sold Joseph. The worst view of Judah's motives is that he was motivated primarily by a desire to get some money out of this and cared nothing for Joseph. After all, being sold as a slave into Egypt could prove a death sentence for young Joseph. Whatever his motives, Judah's arguments persuaded the others.

> **28 And there passed by Midianites merchantmen; and they drew and lifted up Joseph out of the pit, and sold Joseph to the Ishmeelites for twenty pieces of silver: and they brought Joseph into Egypt.**

This verse has been interpreted in more than one way. Some see two different groups of traders. According to this view, while the brothers were preoccupied, some Midianites pulled Joseph out and later sold him to Ishmeelites. In other words, the word "they" referred to the Midianites, not to the brothers.

The more traditional view is that the Midianites and the Ishmaelites were two names for the same group. The names are used this way in Judges 8:22, 24. The "they" would then be the brothers, who carried through with Judah's suggestion and sold Joseph for twenty pieces of silver.

5. Plan 4: cover-up (37:29–32)

Reuben had not been present during the action recorded in verses 25–28. When he found the pit empty, he was so upset that he tore his clothes (37:29). He wondered aloud about what was going to happen (37:30). The brothers put into action their earlier cover-up plan (37:20). They smeared Joseph's coat with the blood of one of the kids from their flock (37:31). Then they went home and told Jacob that they had found this blood-stained coat. They asked Jacob if it was Joseph's coat (37:32).

6. Jacob's grief (37:33–35)

Jacob immediately recognized the blood-stained coat as Joseph's. He assumed that a wild animal had killed and eaten Joseph (37:33). Jacob then went into deep mourning for many days (37:34). All his sons and daughters (probably included daughters-in-law) tried to comfort Jacob, but he refused to be comforted. He vowed to go to his grave still mourning for Joseph (37:35).

SUMMARY OF BIBLE TRUTHS

1. Parental favoritism leads to many family problems.
2. Unresolved hatred can lead to violence.
3. Murder is a terrible crime.
4. Indifference to the cries of others reveals a hard heart.
5. Some money is gained at a terrible price.
6. Some of the worst attitudes and actions take place within the same family.

APPLYING THE BIBLE

1. Lucky dog? I saw the following notice on a bulletin board some time ago. I hope it was a spoof! "Lost: Big black dog in the Sunshine Mall area. One ear bitten off; brown spots on back due to mange; walks around with a bad limp due to a broken front leg; cut on face above nose; no collar; no tag; part of tail missing. Answers to the name *Lucky*." At one point Joseph's life sounded a lot like he was kin to Lucky! With friends like his, the honest man must have asked, who needs enemies? All men have experienced being hated without a cause. The Psalmist certainly knew that affliction.

In Psalm 35:7 he says, "For without cause have they hid for me their net in a pit, which without cause they have digged for my soul."

Later, in the same Psalm (v. 19) he says that some "hate me without a cause."

In Psalm 69:4, he says, "They that hate me without a cause are more than the hairs of mine head: they that would destroy me, being mine enemies wrongfully, are mighty. . ."

In Psalm 7:4, he says, "I have delivered him that without cause is mine enemy." "A brother is born for adversity" (Prov. 17:17) but not to produce it! But Jesus warned, surely remembering Joseph's story, that "a brother shall deliver up the brother to death" (Matt. 10:21).

2. The set of the sail. Perhaps the key virtue of Joseph's life was his refusal to retaliate against those who hurt him. His soul was sailing in a different direction.

> One ship drives east and another drives west
> With the selfsame winds that blow.
> 'Tis the set of the sails
> And not the gales
> Which tell us the way to go.
> Like the winds of the sea are the winds of fate,
> As we voyage along through life,
> 'Tis the set of the soul
> That decides its goal.
> And not the calm or the strife.[1]

3. Different production. Another way of putting it is to recall a story that came out of the Berlin wall days. The East Germans developed a habit of throwing rotting garbage over a section of the wall into West Germany. The West Germans discussed the matter and decided to toss fresh flowers over the wall in response, with this note attached to every bundle: "You give us what you produce; we give you what we produce."

4. Above and below. Notice that Joseph's problems began with his own brothers. That is certainly not an unusual thing. One remembers the same thing happening to others: Abel, Isaac, Jacob, and even to our Lord Himself.

> To live above with those we know,
> That will be glory;
> To live below with those we know,
> That's another story!

But the home is the laboratory of life; one must make every effort to make the faith functional there. Joseph did.

5. Making good at home. "When an American soldier in France won the Croix de Guerre, he refused to wear it. When asked why he did not wear it proudly as he should, the soldier explained, 'I was no good back home. I let my sister and my widowed mother support me. I was a deadbeat. And now they have given me the Croix de Guerre for something I did at the front. I am not going to put it on. I am going back home first. I am going to win there. I am going to show my mother that I can make good at home. Then I will put on the Croix de Guerre.' He is the the first to have discovered that being heroic in a crisis is sometimes even easier than being useful at home."[2]

6. For discussion:

- Why is the home a fruitful source of problems relating to personality differences?
- Why are home-centered problems so difficult to resolve?
- What special advantages, if any, exist in home settings for resolving differences?
- How could one home, in your view, have produced such different children as that of Joseph's?
- Why is it so necessary for one person—such as Joseph in our study for today—to take the initiative in resolving differences?
- Why is it so important, as a testimony before the world, that we resolve destructive differences in our faith families (our churches) as well as in our flesh families (our homes)?

TEACHING THE BIBLE

- *Main Idea:* Joseph's move from favored son to a slave describes the experience of many.
- *Suggested Teaching Aim:* To lead adults to analyze why family relationships break down and to identify steps they will take to prevent this.

A TEACHING OUTLINE

From Favored Son to Slave—Genesis 37:1–35

1. *The Hatred of Joseph's Brothers (37:1–11)*
2. *The Evil Actions of Joseph's Brothers (37:12–35)*

Introduce the Bible Study

Use the ad in illustration #1 from "Applying the Bible" to introduce the lesson. Point out that in today's lesson Joseph went from feeling lucky to feeling quite miserable.

Search for Biblical Truth

Since the background passage covers a large amount of text, number and copy the seven summary statements in "Outline and Summary" and ask two readers to read them aloud alternately.

IN ADVANCE, without moving chairs, ask a third of the class to listen for ways *Israel* (or Jacob) contributed to the breakdown of the family, a third to listen for ways *Joseph* contributed, and a third for ways the *brothers* contributed. Distribute paper and pencils for members to record ideas.

IN ADVANCE, copy "A Teaching Outline" on a large sheet of paper. Cover the two points with strips of paper until you are ready to teach them. Uncover the first point at this time and ask a volunteer to read aloud Genesis 37:3–4. Ask members to read different translations of 37:3 to describe Joseph's coat. Say, whatever it was, the coat was not designed for work but served to separate Joseph from his brothers.

DISCUSS: How can parental favoritism lead to family problems?

Uncover the second point on the outline and ask a volunteer to read aloud 37:17. On a map of the Old Testament, locate Shechem and Dothan. On a chalkboard write:

Plan 1.—
Plan 2.—
Plan 3.—

Ask members to open their Bibles to 37:18–20 and identify what the brothers' first plan was. (To kill Joseph.) Write this opposite **Plan 1.** Ask: How do you think the brothers recognized him from a distance? (Possibly his coat.) What reason did the brothers give for killing him? (He was a dreamer.)

DISCUSS: How has unresolved hatred influenced your life?

Ask members to look at 37:21–24. Ask: What was Reuben's plan? (Put Joseph in a dry cistern.) Write this on the chalkboard opposite **Plan 2**. Ask: Why do you think Reuben suggested this action? Was Reuben part of the conspiracy? (Probably not; he "heard" about it.)

DISCUSS: How does indifference to the cries of family members lead to destruction?

Ask members to look at 37:25–28. Ask: What was Judah's plan? (Sell Joseph.) Write this opposite **Plan 3.** Why did he not want to kill Joseph? (They would have Joseph's blood on their hands.) To whom and by whom was Joseph sold? (See discussion in "Studying the Bible.")

DISCUSS: How do we sell out family members today?

Briefly summarize how the brothers tried to cover up their crime.

Give the Truth a Personal Focus

Call for the three groups to share how each person contributed to the problem. Write their suggestions on a chalkboard. Read aloud the six statements in "Summary of Bible Truths." Add any of these statements that members did not mention to the above list.

Ask members to respond silently: Do you recognize any of your own destructive behavior in this list? What steps can you do to correct this? Allow time for silent prayer and confession.

---

1. Quoted in *Believe,* edited by Richard M. Devos (Old Tappan, N.J.: Fleming H. Revell Company, 1975), 107.

2. Harry Emerson Fosdick, quoted in *The Great American Bathroom Book,* vol. 3 (Salt Lake City: Compact Classics, 1991), 490.

Opportunity to Serve

Background Passage: Genesis 39:1–41:57

Focal Passages: Genesis 41:14–16, 25–27, 34–40

Faithfulness often is rewarded with opportunities to serve God and others. Jacob was faithful in Potiphar's house, and he ended up in prison. He was faithful in prison, but he seemed to have been forgotten. Then Pharaoh's dream provided his big opportunity. As a result, God used Joseph not only to save Egypt but also to save Israel and all his family.

▶**Study Aim:** *To describe Joseph's opportunity to serve.*

STUDYING THE BIBLE

OUTLINE AND SUMMARY

   I. **Joseph's Faithfulness (Gen. 39:1–40:23)**
      1. **Faithful in Potiphar's house (39:1–20)**
      2. **Faithful in prison (39:21–40:23)**
  II. **Joseph's Big Opportunity (Gen. 41:1–57)**
      1. **Opportunity to interpret Pharaoh's dream (41:1–24)**
      2. **Interpretation of the dream (41:25–32)**
      3. **Opportunity to advise Pharaoh (41:33–36)**
      4. **Opportunity to administer the plan (41:37–45)**
      5. **Joseph's administration of the plan (41:46–57)**

Joseph was faithful to God in Potiphar's house, but the false accusations of Potiphar's wife sent him to prison (39:1–20). He was faithful in prison, but seemed to have been forgotten (39:21–40:23). His big opportunity came when Pharaoh sent for Joseph to interpret his disturbing dream (41:1–24). Joseph interpreted the dream as something God was about to do (41:25–32) and advised Pharaoh what to do about it (41:33–36). Pharaoh was so impressed that he appointed Joseph to administer his proposal (41:37–45). Thus, at age thirty, Joseph began to administer the plan (41:46–57).

I. Joseph's Faithfulness (Gen. 39:1–40:23)

1. Faithful in Potiphar's house (39:1–20)

When Joseph was brought to Egypt as a slave, he was sold to Potiphar, one of Pharaoh's officers (39:1). Because the Lord was with Joseph, he soon proved himself such a diligent and trustworthy servant that Potiphar entrusted the running of his household to Joseph (39:2–6). When Potiphar's wife tried to seduce Joseph, he refused and fled from her grasp (39:7–12). She accused Joseph of trying to rape her, and Joseph was thrown into prison (39:13–20).

2. Faithful in prison (39:21–40:23)

Because the Lord was with Joseph in prison, the prison keeper trusted Joseph to run things (39:21–23). Meanwhile, Pharaoh's butler and baker offended Pharaoh, were imprisoned, and were placed under Joseph's care (40:1–4). The butler and the baker each had disturbing dreams (40:5). Joseph was careful to insist that the interpretation of dreams was from God; therefore, he asked them to tell him their dreams (40:6–8). He interpreted the butler's dream that he would be set free in three days (40:9–13). Joseph told the butler of his own plight and asked the butler to bring his case to Pharaoh's attention (40:14–15). The meaning of the baker's dream was that he would be executed in three days (40:16–19). Joseph's interpretations came true, but the butler forgot Joseph (40:20–23).

II. Joseph's Big Opportunity (Gen. 41:1–57)

1. Opportunity to interpret Pharaoh's dream (41:1–24)

14 Then Pharaoh sent and called Joseph, and they brought him hastily out of the dungeon: and he shaved himself, and changed his raiment, and came in unto Pharaoh.

15 And Pharaoh said unto Joseph, I have dreamed a dream, and there is none that can interpret it: and I have heard say of thee, that thou canst understand a dream to interpret it.

16 And Joseph answered Pharaoh, saying, It is not in me: God shall give Pharaoh an answer of peace.

Joseph had languished in prison for two years after the butler was released. Joseph had been in Egypt many years; and from all outward indications, he was no closer to seeing his own dreams fulfilled than when his brothers had sold him. In spite of his faithfulness and the presence of the Lord with him, he was in prison for being faithful to God.

Then something happened that would provide Joseph with his big opportunity. Joseph later would look back and see the hand of God in all these things. Pharaoh had a disturbing dream that none of his wise men could interpret (41:1–8). Finally the butler remembered Joseph and told Pharaoh about the young Hebrew who had accurately explained his dream and that of the baker (41:9–13).

Pharaoh then called for Joseph to be brought to him. Everyone moved hastily to obey Pharaoh's order. Joseph took time to shave and to change clothes. Since Egyptians were clean shaven, Joseph wanted to look his best.

When Joseph arrived in court, Pharaoh told him that he had had a dream that no one could explain. The king also told Joseph that someone had told him that Joseph could interpret dreams. Joseph quickly denied that he as a human had the power to explain dreams. Joseph testified that only God could do that. However, he added a word of assurance that God intended to give Pharaoh "an answer of peace." This did not mean that the message would contain no bad news. It meant that the long-range results of Pharaoh's dream would result in peace and prosperity.

Joseph was unapologetic in testifying that his powers came from God. Pharaoh, the ruler of the world's greatest empire, had had a dream that neither he nor his wise men could explain; however, God would give them the meaning. This shows the weakness of earthly powers and the sovereign rule of God over all. God was moving in the affairs of nations to accomplish His good purpose.

Pharaoh then told Joseph his two-part dream of the seven fat and lean cattle and the seven full and lean ears of grain. He complained that he had told the dream to his magicians, but none of them had been able to explain the dream (41:17–24).

2. Interpretation of the dream (41:25–32)

> **25 And Joseph said unto Pharaoh, The dream of Pharaoh is one: God hath shewed Pharaoh what he is about to do.**
>
> **26 The seven good kine are seven years; and the seven good ears are seven years: the dream is one.**
>
> **27 And the seven thin and ill favoured kine that came up after them are seven years; and the seven empty ears blasted with the east wind shall be seven years of famine.**

Joseph emphasized that the two parts of Pharaoh's dream were part of one dream. Later he explained that the repetition of the two sets of seven meant that the events were sure to happen according to God's plan (41:32). Joseph made clear that the dreams were sent by God to show Pharaoh what God was about to do.

The two sets of sevens stood for seven years each. God was sending to Egypt seven years of plenty to be followed by seven years of famine (41:28–32). All of this was part of God's plan, which only became apparent later. The revelation by God of what He was about to do shows not only God's sovereign power to do it but also His mercy in providing opportunity for Pharaoh and others to prepare for the crisis. Of course, as subsequent verses show, these events provided faithful Joseph with his big opportunity to serve God and others.

3. Opportunity to advise Pharaoh (41:33–36)

> **34 Let Pharaoh do this, and let him appoint officers over the land, and take up the fifth part of the land of Egypt in the seven plenteous years.**
>
> **35 And let them gather all the food of those good years that come, and lay up corn under the hand of Pharaoh, and let them keep food in the cities.**
>
> **36 And that food shall be for store to the land against the seven years of famine, which shall be in the land of Egypt; that the land perish not through the famine.**

Joseph not only interpreted the meaning of the dream but also advised Pharaoh what to do to handle the crisis. No doubt the advice also came from the Lord, not from the mind of Joseph. The Hebrew advised Pharaoh first to name someone to administer the program he was about to outline. That person should be "wise and discreet," and he should be given responsibility for all Egypt (41:33). Then Pharaoh should appoint officers to serve with the overseer of the entire land.

Many Bible students assume that the "fifth part" referred to a fifth part of the produce, which was to be set aside each year. Other Bible students, however, point out that the text says "the fifth part of the land of Egypt." They suggest that the meaning is that the land of Egypt was to be divided into five districts for the purpose of administering this program. We also need to recognize that the word translated "corn" meant "grain of any kind," not the grain that Americans call "corn." Whatever the meaning of "fifth part," the main features of the plan are clear to us. During the seven good years, as much as possible of the rich harvests was to be stored for future use. This was to be done under the authority of Pharaoh.

Not only were the main features clear, but so was its purpose. Joseph pointed out that the purpose of God was "that the land of Egypt perish not through the famine." Here is clear evidence of God's goodness and mercy. In working out His plan to preserve the chosen people of Israel, God also saved Egypt from starvation.

4. Opportunity to administer the plan (41:37–45)

37 And the thing was good in the eyes of Pharaoh, and in the eyes of all his servants.

38 And Pharaoh said unto his servants, Can we find such a one as this is, a man in whom the spirit of God is?

39 And Pharaoh said unto Joseph, Forasmuch as God hath shewed thee all this, there is none so discreet and wise as thou art:

40 Thou shalt be over my house, and according unto thy word shall all my people be ruled: only in the throne will I be greater than thee.

Pharaoh was impressed by Joseph and by what he said. So were the other members of Pharaoh's court. Several things about Joseph probably impressed them. Obviously, they were impressed by Joseph's ability to interpret Pharaoh's dream. Joseph was humble: He did not take credit for himself, but gave it to his God. Joseph showed courage in delivering bad news to Pharaoh about a coming famine, but he offered confident hope about the seven good years. Above all, Joseph not only explained the dream, he also outlined a plan about how to handle the coming crisis.

Pharaoh's words reveal that he considered Joseph "wise and discreet" and a man in whom "the spirit of God" dwelt. The word translated "discreet" means "discerning." When God gave Solomon the opportunity to ask for anything, he asked for "an understanding heart to judge thy people, that I may discern between good and bad" (1 Kings 3:9). God used the two words in Genesis 41:33, 39 to describe the "wise and . . . understanding heart" He had given to Solomon (1 Kings 3:12).

Pharaoh probably did not mean by the "spirit of God" all that the Bible teaches about God's Spirit, but he recognized a supernatural power at work in Joseph. Pharaoh spoke more than he knew. God's Spirit was at work in and through Joseph.

Pharaoh announced that he could never find anyone more well qualified to administer the grain program than Joseph himself. Therefore, he appointed him to a position in Egypt second only in power to Pharaoh. He signified this shared power by placing his ring on Joseph's hand, by riding around with Joseph is a second chariot immediately behind Pharaoh's chariot, and by giving Joseph an Egyptian name and an Egyptian wife (41:44–45).

5. Joseph's administration of the plan (41:46–57)

Joseph was thirty years old when he appeared before Pharoah (41:46). During the next seven years, he diligently administered the plan for storing grain (41:47–49). During those years he had two sons, Ephraim and Manasseh (41:50–52). When the famine began, people cried out to Pharaoh, who sent them to Joseph (41:53–55). Since the famine was not confined to Egypt, people from other lands came to Egypt to buy grain (41:56–57).

SUMMARY OF BIBLE TRUTHS

1. Faithfulness often results in greater opportunities to serve God and others.
2. God moves in the affairs of nations to accomplish His purpose.
3. God's purpose is good.
4. God often uses human instruments to accomplish His purpose.
5. Wisdom and discernment are gifts of God.

APPLYING THE BIBLE

1. How many "Josephs"? Because Joseph gave his life in sacrificial service to others, his name has come down to us with a fragrance that has lasted now for thousands of years. How many "Josephs" are there, and in how many languages, on the earth?

"Through his sorrow, Kunta was surprised to hear that the old gardener had been called 'Josephus.' He wondered what the gardener's true name had been—the name of his African forefathers—and to what tribe they had belonged. He wondered if the gardener himself had known. Most likely he had died as he had lived—without ever learning who he really was."[1]

Without defending the imposition of "Christian" names on slaves, the old gardener could not have worn a more noble name than that of Josephus, after our Old Testament Joseph. Indeed, it is sad if he never knew his "native" name, but sadder still if he never knew, and admired, his biblical namesake.

2. Service. "Everybody can be great . . . because anybody can serve. You don't have to have a college degree to serve. You don't have to make your subject and verb agree to serve. You only need a heart full of grace. A soul generated by love."[2]

3. How far he might jump. I love the story about the young man who was working on a railroad crew one hot summer. He had just finished high school and had chosen not to go to college. One hot day, at lunch time, he dropped his tools and trudged across the field to a small liberal arts college and asked the registrar for a college handbook, indicating he might be interested in enrolling. She handed him one and, with a warning about the challenge of college work, dismissed him with a wave of her hand. Four years later he walked into her office and, showing her his finished transcript of all requirements for graduation, asked her what she thought. She smiled and said, "Well, I think that when you see a bullfrog on a lily-pad, you never know how far he might jump!" Who could have guessed Joseph would have jumped so far!

4. Joseph and Christ. "Joseph stands out among the patriarchs in some respects with preeminence. His nobility of character, his purity of heart and life, his magnanimity as a ruler and a brother make him, more than any other of the Old Testament characters. Joseph is not in the list of persons distinctly referred to as types of Christ—the only perfectly safe criterion—but none more fully illustrates the life and work of the Savior. He wrought salvation for those who betrayed and rejected him, he went down into humiliation as the way to his exaltation, he forgave those who, at least in spirit, put him to death, and to him as to the Savior, all must come for relief, or perish."[3]

5. Doing good and building character. Joseph's noble character produced loving service to others, but his character was, in the process, further developed. There is a correlation between doing good and building character. As Elizabeth Barrett Browning said:

> Thy love shall chant its own beatitudes
> After its own life workings;
> A child's kiss set on thy sighing lips shall make thee glad;
> A poor man helped by thee shall make thee rich;
> A sick man nursed by thee shall give thee health;
> A weak one helped by thee shall give thee strength;
> An ignorant one taught by thee shall make thee wise;
> Thou shalt be served thyself
> By every sense of service which thou renderest![4]

6. About doing good.

> Do all the good you can,
> By all the means you can,
> In all the places you can,
> At all the times you can,
> To all the people you can,
> As long as ever you can.
> —Anonymous

7. Prescription for crisis. There is always a crisis! But God always watches over His own in the crisis.

> "Careless seems the great Avenger;
> History's page but record
> One death-grapple in the darkness
> 'Twixt old system and the Word;
> Truth forever on the scaffold,
> Wrong forever on the throne,—
> Yet that scaffold sways the future,
> And, behind the dim unknown,
> Standeth God within the shadows,
> Keeping watch above his own."
> —James Russell Lowell, "The Present Crisis"

8. For discussion:

▶ Can those craving authority be trusted with it? Always? Sometimes? Never?

▶ Are we always aware of God's providential care?

▶ How can we be sure He does watch over us? What is the proof of His watchcare?

▶ Does the fact that He watches over us immunize us from painful experiences?

▶ Why is it so difficult to trust God through the dark and painful experiences?

▶ Is God under any obligation to explain the reason for the painful experiences to us? Or His plan in them?

TEACHING THE BIBLE

▶ *Main Idea:* Our opportunities to some degree are always built on our past faithfulness.

▶ *Suggested Teaching Aim:* To lead adults to commit themselves to be faithful in whatever task they find themselves.

A TEACHING OUTLINE

Joseph's Big Opportunity (41:1–57)

1. *Opportunity to Interpret Pharaoh's Dreams (41:1–24)*
2. *Interpretation of the Dream (41:25–32)*
3. *Opportunity to Advise Pharaoh (41:33–36)*
4. *Opportunity to Administer the Plan (41:37–45)*

Introduce the Bible Study

Use illustration #3 from "Applying the Bible" to introduce the lesson. Say, Not even Joseph knew how far he would jump when he was sold into slavery.

Search for Biblical Truth

IN ADVANCE, enlist two members to summarize the two subpoints under "I. Joseph's Faithfulness." Give them a copy of the material in "Studying the Bible." As an alternative, enlist a member to do a monologue of Joseph from the time he was sold into slavery until he was brought before Pharaoh.

Read the "Main Idea": "Our opportunities to some degree are always built on our past faithfulness." Ask members why they would agree or disagree with this statement.

IN ADVANCE, copy the title and four points of "A Teaching Outline" on five strips of paper. Place the title on the focal wall. Add the first point.

Ask members to open their Bibles to Genesis 41:14–16 and skim these verses. Ask members to find the answer to these questions in these verses: (1) What specific incident gave Joseph his big break? (Pharaoh's dream.) (2) What in these verses reflects Joseph's spiritual maturity? ("It is not in me: God shall give.") Do you think Joseph took a risk when he testified to Pharaoh about God? Why?

Ask members to skim 41:25–27. Ask: According to these verses, how did Joseph witness for God to the pharaoh? (Said God was in charge of sending dreams and also in charge of the world's weather and economy.) How did this dream show God's mercy? (Allowed Egyptians to prepare for famine.)

Ask members to skim 41:34–36. Ask, What was Joseph's plan for Egypt? (Appoint an administrator to store food during the seven good years.) How much food did Joseph suggest storing? (Likely one-fifth of the crop.) Do you think Joseph had any idea that Pharaoh would appoint him to administer the program?

Ask members to skim 41:37–45. Ask, What do you think impressed Pharaoh to appoint Joseph? (Among other reasons: Joseph's ability to interpret dreams, his humility, his courage to deliver bad news to Pharaoh, his ability to deliver a plan to overcome the problem, and Pharaoh sensed that Joseph was a man in whom was "the spirit of God.") What do you think Joseph felt, having awakened that morning in prison but going to sleep that night as second in command to the pharaoh?

Give the Truth a Personal Focus

Read the following five statements and ask members if they agree or disagree and why. Then ask the follow-up questions.

1. *Faithfulness often results in greater opportunities to serve God and others.* Ask, How has this statement proven true in your life?
2. *God moves in the affairs of nations to accomplish His purpose.* Ask, What evidence can you cite to prove this statement?
3. *God's purpose is good.* Ask, If God's purpose is always good, why do so many bad things happen to us?
4. *God often uses human instruments to accomplish His purpose.* Ask, Have you ever felt you were an instrument to accomplish God's purpose?
5. *Wisdom and discernment are gifts of God.* Ask, Who do you feel has received the gift of wisdom and discernment?

Suggest that Joseph's faithfulness in the long years in which he was a slave and in prison created for him the big opportunity. Encourage members to commit themselves to be faithful in whatever task they find themselves so they will be ready for God's big opportunity.

---

1. Alex Haley, *Roots* (Garden City, N.Y.: Doubleday and Co., 1976), 357.

2. Martin Luther King, Jr., in *The Great American Bathroom Book,* vol. 3 (Salt Lake City: Compact Classics, 1991), 441.

3. *The International Standard Bible Encyclopedia*, vol. III, ed. James Orr (Grand Rapids: Wm. B. Eerdmans Publishing Co., 1955), 1740.

4. Quoted in R. G. Lee, *From Feet to Fathoms* (Orlando, Fla.: Christ for the World Publishers, 1926), 43.

Forgiven and Reunited

Background Passage: Genesis 42:1–45:28
Focal Passages: Genesis 44:18–20, 33–45:7

The climax of the story of Joseph focuses on three key Bible teachings: giving oneself for others, forgiving those who have hurt us, and trusting God to bring some good out of evil. Judah offered to take the punishment of his brother Benjamin. Joseph showed an amazing willingness to forgive the worst kind of betrayal and evil done to him by his brothers. He became convinced that God had been able to weave their evil actions into the fabric of His good purpose for Israel and all his family.

▶**Study Aim:** *To explain how this story illustrates self-giving love, human forgiveness, and divine providence.*

STUDYING THE BIBLE

OUTLINE AND SUMMARY

I.   **Joseph Tested His Brothers (Gen. 42:1–44:34)**
   1. **Joseph's brothers in Egypt (42:1–8)**
   2. **Joseph's accusation of the brothers (42:9–13)**
   3. **Joseph's insistence that they bring Benjamin (42:14–38)**
   4. **Joseph's threat to make Benjamin his slave (43:1–44:17)**
   5. **Judah's plea to take Benjamin's place (44:18–34)**
II. **Joseph Welcomed His Brothers (Gen. 45:1–28)**
   1. **Joseph's revelation (45:1–4)**
   2. **Joseph's explanation (45:5–8)**
   3. **Joseph's instructions (45:9–28)**

When Joseph's brothers came to buy grain in Egypt, Joseph recognized them; but they did not recognize him (42:1–8). Joseph accused them of being spies (42:9–13). He kept Simeon as a hostage and told them he would believe them only when they brought Benjamin to Egypt (42:14–38). Joseph set Benjamin up as if he were guilty of theft and said that Benjamin would be punished by becoming his slave (43:1–44:17). Judah begged to be allowed to take Benjamin's punishment (44:18–24). Joseph then made himself known to them, but they were stunned into silence (45:1–4). Joseph told them not to be afraid because God had used their evil to accomplish His good purpose (45:5–8). He sent them to bring his father Jacob (Israel) and all his family to Egypt (45:9–28).

I. Joseph Tested His Brothers (Gen. 42:1–44:34)

1. Joseph's brothers in Egypt (42:1–8)

Although Jacob kept Benjamin at home, he sent his other sons to Egypt to buy grain (42:1–5). When the ten brothers came, Joseph recognized them; but they did not recognize him (42:6–8).

2. Joseph's accusation of the brothers (42:9–13)

Joseph accused them of being spies (42:9–10). When the brothers tried to refute this accusation, they spoke of their father, their brother who was no more, and their younger brother (42:11–13).

3. Joseph's insistence that they bring Benjamin (42:14–38)

Joseph told them they could prove their innocence only by returning with their younger brother; meanwhile, he would keep one of them as a hostage (42:14–20). Joseph wept after he overheard the brothers saying that they were suffering for the blood of Joseph (42:21–24). Having retained Simeon as the hostage, Joseph told his servants to put the money back in their sacks (42:25). When they discovered the money, the brothers wondered what God was doing to them (42:26–28). When they told Jacob (42:29–35), he complained that the brothers had taken Joseph and Simeon from him; and he said that he would never allow Benjamin to go to Egypt (42:37–38).

4. Joseph's threat to make Benjamin his slave (43:1–44:17)

Eventually, Jacob was forced to tell his sons to return to Egypt (43:1–2). When the brothers reminded Jacob of Joseph's demand to see Benjamin, Jacob asked why they had told the man of Benjamin (43:3–7). After Judah pledged to be surety for Benjamin, Jacob saw that he had no choice but to send Benjamin; however, he sent gifts, returned double the money, and asked God to return all his sons safely (43:8–14).

When the brothers arrived in Egypt, they were invited to Joseph's house, where they were reunited with Simeon (43:15–23). During the meal, Joseph asked about the health of their elderly father and left the room to weep when he looked at Benjamin (43:24–34). Joseph ordered that his silver cup be placed in Benjamin's sack, had the brothers retained and accused, and brought them back before him (44:1–13). Joseph told the others that they were free to go, but that Benjamin must become his slave (44:14–17).

5. Judah's plea to take Benjamin's place (44:18–34)

18 Then Judah came near unto him, and said, Oh, my lord, let thy servant, I pray thee, speak a word in my lord's ears, and let not thine anger burn against thy servant: for thou art even as Pharaoh.

19 My lord asked his servants saying, Have ye a father, or a brother?

20 And we said unto my lord, We have a father, an old man, and a child of his old age, a little one; and his brother is dead, and he alone is left of his mother, and his father loveth him.

33 Now therefore, I pray thee, let thy servant abide instead of the lad a bondsman to my lord; and let the lad go up with his brethren.

34 For how shall I go up to my father, and the lad be not with me? lest peradventure I see the evil that shall come on my father.

Judah's speech in verses 18–34 is one of the most powerful in the Bible. Much of it consisted of quotations of what they, Joseph, or their father had said. Joseph had asked about their family, and they had told him the truth. Notice how Judah described Jacob, Joseph, and Benjamin in verse 20. For the first time, the brothers spoke of Joseph as being dead. Earlier, both they and Jacob had spoken of him as being "no more" (42:13, 32, 36). However, in their words of remorse spoken to one another, but overheard by Joseph, Reuben spoke of "his blood" being required of them (42:22).

Joseph's test was designed to see if the brothers felt any guilt over what they had done to him and to determine if they would do the same thing again if the situation arose. He had seen signs of their remorse over their sin against him.

Most of all, Judah's speech shows a deepened love and respect for their aging father and thus for Benjamin, whom Jacob loved so dearly. Judah emphasized this love by describing Benjamin as the child of Jacob's old age, the only surviving son of his most loved wife, and his beloved son. They had seen what their report of the death of Joseph had done to their father, and Judah was determined not to inflict any further pain on the old man.

Judah recounted the conversations with Jacob about taking Benjamin to Egypt. The emphasis throughout is on Jacob's great love for Benjamin and on how it would kill him if anything happened to his beloved son (44:21–31). Judah told Joseph that he had become surety for his brother (44:32). Therefore, Judah begged Joseph to let Judah fulfill that promise to his father by taking his brother's place. In other words, Judah would become the slave of Joseph so that Benjamin might be set free to return to his father. Judah said that he personally could not bear to go back without Benjamin and to see the evil results on Jacob.

Judah is one of the Bible's best examples of two things: how a life can be transformed and how one person can give himself for others. This was surely a different kind of Judah than the brother who proposed the plan of selling Joseph as a slave (37:26–27). God had used his father's faith and grief to transform him into one who was willing to give himself in the place of his brother. Christians see in Judah a foreshadowing of the ultimate self-giving of Jesus, who on the human side was a descendant of Judah.

II. Joseph Welcomed His Brothers (Gen. 45:1–28)

1. Joseph's revelation (45:1–4)

1 Then Joseph could not refrain himself before all them that stood by him; and he cried, Cause every man to go out from me. And there stood no man with him, while Joseph made himself known unto his brethren.

2 And he wept aloud: and the Egyptians and the house of Pharaoh heard.

3 And Joseph said unto his brethren, I am Joseph; doth my father yet live? And his brethren could not answer him; for they were troubled at his presence.

4 And Joseph said unto his brethren, Come near to me, I pray you. And they came near. And he said, I am Joseph your brother, whom ye sold into Egypt.

Joseph dismissed his Egyptian servants in order to have this private time with his brothers. Then he wept so loudly that he was overheard by the Egyptians and by those in Pharaoh's house. Then addressing his brothers, he said, "I am Joseph." He also asked if his father was still alive. Earlier they had told him that Jacob was alive. Joseph may have been looking for reassurance, or he may have simply been too overcome with emotion to know what to say.

As far as the brothers were concerned, they were too stunned and scared to say anything. Throughout all their dealings with this mighty man of Egypt, they never had any thought that this might be Joseph. Over twenty years had passed. Joseph was no longer seventeen but thirty-nine. He was dressed as an Egyptian. He was second only to Pharaoh in the land. This was a far cry from the hated younger brother whom they had last seen being carried as a slave to Egypt. Also up to this point, the Egyptian had given not the slightest hint that he was Joseph. Now suddenly the man announced that he was Joseph!

Joseph told them to come near, where they could get a better look at him. And then, Joseph told them something that only Joseph would know, "I am Joseph, whom you sold into Egypt."

2. Joseph's explanation (45:5–8)

5 Now therefore be not grieved, nor angry with yourselves, that ye sold me hither: for God did send me before you to preserve life.

6 For these two years hath the famine been in the land: and yet there are five years, in the which there shall neither be earing nor harvest.

7 And God sent me before you to preserve you a posterity in the earth, and to save your lives by a great deliverance.

Seeing their distress, Joseph tried to reassure them that he was not about to get even with them. He was certainly in an ideal position to do so, and this would have been the normal human response to what they had done to him. Instead Joseph offered them forgiveness and reconciliation. Although the word *forgiveness* is not in this passage, it is spelled out in a scene after Jacob died (Gen. 50:17–19).

Joseph is not only a model of forgiveness but also of trust in the goodness of God. Joseph could have become angry and bitter toward God. Instead, he continued to trust God and to be faithful to God throughout all his trials and temptations in Egypt. As he reflected on his experience, Joseph came to believe that God had been able to weave even their evil actions into the fabric of His good purpose to deliver His people.

Verses 5, 7–8 are strong statements of faith in God's ability to work all things together for good for those who love Him (Rom. 8:28). Their evil actions had sent Joseph into Egypt, where God had led him to a position in which he had the power and resources to see that Israel and his family would survive the famine. After all, as he told his brothers, five more years of famine still lay ahead.

Just as we see Judah as a foreshadowing of Jesus, so do we see Joseph in the same way. He showed the kind of forgiving spirit that Jesus had.

And God used the evil done to Joseph and his faithfulness in sufferings to foreshadow the cross. Human sin and divine love collided there, and out of it God offers salvation to all people. Joseph did not intend his words to excuse his brothers of their guilt or to take sin lightly. Neither does the cross.

3. Joseph's instructions (45:9–28)

Joseph's treatment of them showed his forgiveness and reconciliation. He told the brothers to return and tell Jacob that Joseph was alive and urge him to bring all his family to Egypt, where they would be given a special place to live and food to eat (45:9–12). He hugged them and wept for joy with all eleven of his brothers (45:13–15). When Pharaoh heard about this reunion, he added his authority to reinforce what Joseph had said (45:16–20). Joseph loaded them down with gifts and sent them to tell Jacob the good news (45:21–24). Jacob at first could not believe news that seemed too good to be true (45:25–26). When his sons explained, Jacob prepared for this joyful reunion with Joseph (45:27–28).

SUMMARY OF BIBLE TRUTHS

1. Giving yourself for others is the highest kind of love.
2. Forgiving terrible evil is another high expression of love.
3. God can work out His good purpose in the face of evil actions and human suffering.
4. The cross is the ultimate expression of self giving, forgiveness, and divine providence.
5. Trusting God when your faithfulness seems to bring only suffering is a high level of faith.
6. God's ability to work all things together for good does not minimize evil or excuse sin.

APPLYING THE BIBLE

1. Serindipity. A word entered the English language in 1754 that has since become popular. It is the word *serendipity*. It refers to the experience of being pleasantly surprised, "out of the blue," in an unexpected way. It was introduced into the language by Horace Walpole, who had found it in a Persian story, "The Three Princes of Serendip." Three men, in their travels, were always blessed by "chance" happenings.

Perhaps in no man's life in the Bible is the leading of God more obvious than that of Joseph. It was as if God was leading every step through the struggles of his life—as indeed He was! This was not just natural serendipity, however. It was supernatural providence—not luck but the Lord; not happenstance but heaven!

2. Serving others. Joseph's life was given in service to others. Think on these things:

▶ "Real friends are those who, when you've made a fool of yourself, don't feel you've done a permanent job" (Anonymous).

▶ "What do we live for, if it is not to make life less difficult for each other?" (George Eliot).

▶ "There is no beautifier of complexion, or form, or behaviour, like the wish to scatter joy and not pain around us" (Ralph Waldo Emerson).

▶ "You can make more friends in two months by becoming interested in other people than you can in two years by trying to get other people interested in you" (Dale Carnegie).

3. A random act of kindness. On the morning I write these lines, I read, earlier, a touching story of forgiveness. An American boy, seven years old, was traveling in Italy with his family when the family's car was ravaged by masked assailants on a remote Italian road. The boy was hit in the head, fell into a coma, and was declared brain-dead. "His parents donated his organs in an act that saved seven other lives, inspired a surge of organ donations in a country where such gestures were rare—and turned (the family) into a symbol of generosity." The parents, in their immense grief, have expressed a desire to get on with life and said, "It (the murder) has inspired this outpouring of compassion all over the world, and on a practical level, the increase in donations in organs. Literally hundreds of people are alive because of (our son). When the history of the world comes to be written, I think (our son) will be a shining footnote in it."

4. Seeing the bright side. A priest was robbed, but when his friends offered condolences, his response was that he was a very fortunate man. When they asked how, he said, "First, it was my wallet and not my life that he took; then, there wasn't much in the wallet anyway, and finally, thank God it was he who robbed me and not I who robbed him!"

5. Suffering for whom? "What I want to know is not why I suffer, but only whether I suffer for Thy sake." That proverb reminds me of a visit to a very old gentleman, a member of our church, who was suffering terribly and losing his battle to cancer rapidly. In anguish, he turned to me and said, "Pastor, if I could believe God could make something positive out of my suffering, I could bear it."

6. Belief influences character. Even the atheist Voltaire confessed, "I do, it is true, expect more justice from one who believes in God than from one who has no such belief." After presenting this quotation, raise the following questions for discussion:

▶ Does the worldly man, even an atheist like Voltaire, have such a right? If so, why?

▶ What gives the Christian the ability to show more grace than he was given?

7. Quick quotes. How does Joseph's life relate to the following sentiments by anonymous authors?

▶ "The man who can take abuse with a smile is fit to be a leader."

▶ "Better suffer an injustice than commit one."

▶ "The best morsels are given to the worst dogs."

▶ "An eagle doesn't catch flies."

▶ "No one ever forgets where he buried the hatchet."

▶ "Valor would cease to be a virtue if there were no injustice."

▶ "If I didn't have any bad luck, I wouldn't have any luck at all."

▶ "The world is not fair, but God is more than fair."

TEACHING THE BIBLE

▶ *Main Idea:* Joseph's forgiveness and reunion with his brothers illustrates self-giving love, human forgiveness, and divine providence.

▶ *Suggested Teaching Aim:* To lead adults to analyze how self-giving love, human forgiveness, and divine providence have worked in their lives.

A TEACHING OUTLINE

Forgiven and Reunited

1. *Giving Oneself for Others (Gen. 44:18–20, 33–34)*
2. *Forgiving Those Who Have Hurt Us (Gen. 45:1–4)*
3. *Bringing Good Out of Evil (Gen. 45:5–8)*

Introduce the Bible Study

Use illustration #5 from "Applying the Bible" to introduce the Bible study.

Search for Biblical Truth

IN ADVANCE, copy the title and three points of "A Teaching Outline" on a large sheet of paper. Cover the points with thin strips of paper until you are ready to teach them.

IN ADVANCE, enlist two readers to read the statements in "Studying the Bible" under "Joseph Tested His Brothers" subpoints 1–4 to explain the context. Copy the material and ask the two members to read the sentences alternately.

Uncover the first outline point and read aloud Genesis 44:18–20, 33–34. If your members work well in small groups, organize members into three groups and assign each group one of the following lists to answer. Or lecture briefly, covering these points: (1) Jacob is an old man; (2) for the first time Judah describes Joseph as "dead"; (3) Judah's speech shows deepened love and respect for Jacob and Benjamin; (4) Judah offered himself as surety for Benjamin; (5) Judah exemplifies how a life can be transformed and how one person can give himself for others; (6) Judah foreshadows the ultimate self giving of Jesus, a descendant of Judah.

Uncover the second outline point and read aloud 45:1–5. Lecture briefly, covering these points: (1) Joseph had to convince his brothers who he was; (2) they did not recognize him because it had been twenty-two years since they had seen Joseph, and he was dressed like an Egyptian; (3) to convince them who he was, he told them he was "Joseph, whom you sold into Egypt"—something only Joseph would have known; (4) Joseph encouraged them not to be afraid; he was not going to take vengeance (see 50:17–19).

Uncover the third outline point and read aloud 45:6–7. Lecture briefly, covering these points: (1) Joseph modeled trust in the goodness of God; (2) Joseph believed that God had been able to weave even his brothers' evil actions into the fabric of His good purpose to deliver His people; (3) Joseph believed in God's ability to work all things together for good for those who love Him (Rom. 8:28); (4) Joseph foreshadows the kind of forgiving spirit Jesus had; (5) the evil done to Joseph and his faithfulness in suffering foreshadow the cross. Why?

DISCUSS: Since the brothers' actions of selling Joseph brought about the salvation of Israel, were they wrong to do what they did?

Using the six statements in "Summary of Bible Truths," develop a three- to four-minute lecture by stating each truth and adding a brief explanatory statement to each truth.

Give the Truth a Personal Focus

Ask, Which approach do you think would have been most satisfying to Joseph: forgiveness or revenge? Why? How has self-giving love, human forgiveness, and divine providence worked in your life? Have you been the recipient of any of these? Have you extended them to someone else? How has God worked in your life to bring about His divine providence of using something bad for your good?

Close in prayer that all will allow God to give them the grace to demonstrate self-giving love and human forgiveness and to allow God to use for good what others meant for evil in their lives.